Chapter 1 - Whittle Faeries and the Buurn Folk

In the regions of our world where the weather is a little warmer, in the forests, on the edges of forests, along country streams and fields, like small shining stars; the Whittle Faeries and Buurn Folk would be working away, but are very difficult to see. Most of these species of faeries are between two and six inches in height and they look very, very similar to humans. Many, many thousands of years ago some faeries, including the Whittle and Buurn Folk were related in a way to humans. Only now unfortunately, the faeries are really quite scared of humans and the damage that some are doing to the environment.

Some of these faeries have wings and can fly while some of them do not. The faeries with wings move so quickly that you might only see a tiny ball of golden light when they are flying. A little I suppose like a firefly, but faster and brighter. The faeries without wings do not consider themselves any less lucky as they still have the magical ability to disappear and reappear at will. Who knows where they go to? Sometimes even they do not know where they go, but they never fail to return. It might even be that if a young faerie is still learning how to disappear, the mother will have to go looking for it and bring it back. I wonder, where do you think they might go to?

As with most faeries, the Whittle and Buurn Folk are born in a very special way. When two faeries meet and are very fond of each other, they may decide to give their living energy to make a new baby faerie which is achieved in a simple but beautiful way. The two faeries choose a flower they are associated with and then blow their physical energy into their cupped hands, this is then mixed with energy from the spirit world and placed inside a flower. Sometimes the flower may have to be persuaded to keep it's petals gently closed overnight, although the flowers do understand what is occuring. In the morning a new baby faerie will appear from the flower. For the rest of the faerie's life, it's hair colour and skin colour will match the colour of the flower's stem and petals associated with at birth.

When the faeries are not working in the earth's forest during the warm summer months, you would find them in their village. It is not easy to get to these villages as you need to be taken there by someone, such as a mole faerie. The mole faerie would take you down a small tunnel from the world of humans to the world of faeries. This may be a perfect replica of a village on earth before motor vehicles existed. You might see carriages made of gold being pulled by mice or moles; moles are more popular as their eyesight is not very good, so they follow instructions quite well! The village would be so clean and peaceful, with small cottages of thatched roofs so very similar to cottages in the southern English countryside. Almost everyone would be busy cleaning, doing chores, talking and a few of them riding and steering the carriage. I imagine they would all take turns riding in the carriage and maybe delivering nectar for food. What kind of chores do you think the village faerie would be responsible for?

The faeries use petals from flowers that have dropped to the ground, these petals are coated with a special liquid they produce from their mouth. This process then allows the petals to be wrapped around their skin for clothing and some of the petals are even used to make hats. Can you imagine how pretty and colourful these faeries must be with their green clothing, yellow hair, green skin and bright golden auras? Do you wish you could visit the world of the Whittle and Buurn Folk someday?

Chapter 2 - Sheharnie Faeries

For millions of years faeries have existed, however, not all of them came from planet earth and not all of them started life as physical beings. Many of them were created in the spirit world and lived there before starting life on our earth and other physical planets. Some faeries can even move and live on different planets so when they disappear at will, only the faeries know where they have gone.

The Sheharnies are related to the Buurn Folk and live in the northern wooded areas of our earth. The Sheharnies are a little smaller than the Whittle and Buurn Folk and can choose whether they will appear as a male or female and can change at any time. They are a very sensitive and very wise faerie. They also have a Prima Sheharnie faerie but not all faeries have a Prima faerie. A Prima faerie is a faerie that has learnt to give just that little bit more than a regular faerie, to help improve oneself and in turn help others in need, such as animals and flowers. The Prima Sheharnie has a crystal lodged in it's forehead, this shows the faerie has learnt to give more, the crystal is yellow in colour and becomes brighter at night time. All Sheharnies have the most beautiful pink aura surrounding them, the brighter the aura and crystal, the wiser and more giving they are. Just as you might sacrifice your time to help other children with their homework or with their chores, your aura may grow. Do you think helping others improves all our lives? If you were a Sheharnie faerie, how could you help other faeries?

They have elliptical eyes, pointed ears, fairly small pointed wings on top and small round wings on the bottom and reach about four inches in height. Their lips are a glossy pink with sparkles on them and with hair the colour of black or brown. When they cut their hair they use the leftover hair to weave into baskets, like tiny wicker baskets used to carry bee pollen. The basket uses a small strap between the wings to hold it tight. They use spider thread to stitch petals together to make clothing and hats. The only possession they have is the small sack they carry. They place a much higher value on the ability to give love above all else!

They use squirrels to help them store food, sharing with them since many times the squirrels forget where they buried their nuts. Their lifespan is about fifty of our earth years, after which they return to the spirit world, just as all living beings do. Baby Sheharnie are created the same way as the Whittle and Buurn Folk. Do you remember, by blowing their love energy into a flower? In seven days a new baby Sheharnie appears, and of course the parents always thank the flower. During this period the parents stand by making sure the flower's petals are not opened.

Sheharnies have a reputation for being a little grumpy in the morning, especially if they do not get enough sleep. Now who would have thought that! They are definitely not morning people, but by lunchtime they are as chirpy as a chickadee or a sparrow in springtime. They eat nuts and berries and drink water from small streams. They might even wash in the same stream, as long as the water is not flowing too fast. Clean water is very important to the faeries.

Snails are always one animal they like to tickle with leaves. They spend most of their day gathering just enough supplies for the day, after this they go and play, singing and dancing away. The other faeries consider the Sheharnies a little bit mad, as the Sheharnies love to dance in the rain, trying to catch the raindrops, which can go on for hours at a time. They might live in small nests that other animals or birds have abandoned. Most faeries speak a common language called Kreak. Kreak has twenty six phrases and seventeen dialects. This language is

very adaptable to other human languages and was originally based on all human languages on earth.

Their main focus and purpose is to help the environment. This is achieved by moving seeds from flowers and trees to new areas where they can grow without harm from humans, insecticides or pesticides. You can imagine that this is getting more and more difficult, due to clear-cut logging, pesticides, insecticides and pollution.

Chapter 3 - Fauna Faeries

There are many, many different kinds of Fauna faerie and they are all representing animals. It could be a Cat Fauna faerie, a Gorilla Fauna faerie, a Dinosaur Fauna faerie, a Lion Fauna faerie, a Dog Fauna faerie, a Chinchilla Fauna faerie, a Rabbit Fauna faerie or an Elephant Fauna faerie, the list is very long. For example, the Lion Fauna faerie may look like a lion but may have hands and feet and the lion may wear clothes and even walk upright. There really is no limit to the imagination as to how a Fauna faerie animal may appear. A Hippopotamus Fauna faerie may walk on two legs wearing a waistcoat and top hat, the way they present themselves can be endless. Just use your imagination and try to imagine your favourite animal as a Fauna faerie.

Depending on how they feel they may have hoofs, tails, toes, fingers or wings. They can be male or female, although not all animals will choose to become a Fauna faerie. The ones that do, will try to help animals of their kind on earth that are in need of assistance, such as maybe changing their hunting instincts to survive. What kind of help do you think your favourite animals need?

As an example, a Hare Fauna faerie may have green hair with much smaller ears. When they mix with hares on earth they will change their appearance and become a regular hare so they can blend in more easily. They would still speak in the language that hare use to communicate. Sometimes they will wear clothes but they do not have to have their clothing made, they just use their minds to manifest the clothing they wish to appear. Would it not be nice if we could do this? Because Fauna faerie are usually very happy they tend to make clothing which are bright and colourful.

If you imagine a large dinosaur with wings, that is where the image of a dragon came from. Many years ago a human must have seen a Dinosaur Fauna faerie and then drew a painting of it. A Hippopotamus Fauna faerie would appear much smaller in size and much friendlier, but still with poor eyesight. Because of this the Hippopotamus Fauna faerie tends to be just a little clumsy, always bumping into things.

Fauna faerie from a particular species will all take turns acting as a Beastmaster and setting tasks for the other Fauna faerie. For instance, a zebra may represent the horse species. Giraffes also belong to the horse group and will take turns at being a Beastmaster and setting tasks for others to follow.

Cats and dogs can easily see the different forms of Fauna faerie! At one time, many thousands of years ago humans could also see Fauna faerie. Fauna faerie will try to comfort animals that are part of the food chain before they are killed, helping their spirit return back to the spirit world. It might not seem like much help, but it is the best they can do.

Fauna faerie do eat and drink but do not eat other animals, you will in fact see a Lion Fauna faerie sleeping with a Mouse Fauna faerie or Deer Fauna faerie. Birds are included as Fauna faerie but not fish, fish are from a different species of faeries. When a Fauna faerie has reached a certain level of wisdom or giving, they will then have the ability to grow wings. Fauna faeries such as moles would have difficulty walking on their normal mole feet, so they will have feet more like humans along with better eyesight.

Fauna faerie may be the same size as they were on earth or smaller, such as the hippopotamus. A Goat Fauna faerie may have a goat body for the bottom half and a more human appearance for the top half of it's body. It may walk upright but it may still be covered in a beautiful soft, shiny goatskin over most of it's body.

There are no animals that do not have a Fauna faerie counterpart. Fauna faeries will mix with animals in our homes, but unfortunately they cannot help the poor animals in laboratories that are being experimented on. Can you think of any animals still in this situation? They must wait until the animal departs this life on earth to help them start a recovery period in the spirit world.

Depending on how they feel, Fauna faerie such as an elephant may have red, blue or yellow hair. The more spiritual Fauna faerie species will have a third eye or crystal in their forehead. A horse's crystal would be of a violet colour, gorillas would be blue or even green for the lowland gorillas as they have a healing ability. Chimpanzees are a more violent group on earth and their crystal would be a red colour because of this. Spiders belong to a group of Fauna faerie, but a Fauna faerie Spider would never hurt a fly. Even so, it may make many people nervous to see one, with its eight eyes and maybe using a walking stick. Fauna faerie Spiders are the mathematicians and problems solvers in the Fauna faerie world and are always female.

Bird Fauna faeries have four wings so they don't have to exert so much energy. Which is a big help to birds such as the hummingbird. Eagles are very spiritual, partly because they are so nomadic, their wings will have a spiritual luminosity to it. Tiger Fauna faeries are much more spiritual than lions, the crystal in their forehead will be yellow or green with tiger stripe colours surrounding the single colour. Can you think of three animals and how they might appear if they became a Fauna faerie?

Chapter 4 - Flora Faeries

"To tum te tat ta, tee world and I, per terry a while, by and by, sweet faerie bring thy worlds collide to tum te tat ta, my world and I"

And so we begin the description of the Flora faerie with a line of Kreak, the faerie language.

Flora faeries range in height between two and eight inches and can live up to one hundred and eighty years. They exist on berries and nectar depending on what is available at the time of year, they may even move to warmer areas in winter or in times of extreme cold weather. Their eyes are quite large and are the shape of almonds with the eyelids moving side to side rather than up and down like humans. Their eyes and hair will be the same colour as the flower they come from, for example, a faerie from the Morning Glory flower will have eyes and hair of a powder blue colour.

Their hair if you can believe it has a mind of it's own and you have never seen a bad hair day until you have witnessed the hair belonging to a Flora faerie! Can you imagine having hair that does just as it pleases? You might want the hair to stay a certain way but if the hair decides against this, the hair will always have the last say. This can result in many lengthy discussions on how the faerie would like one's hair to be for the day. Sometimes the hair has to be platted, as the hair will not stay still long enough to be cut or trimmed! Many times when their hair grows very long, the hair will lose some of it's energy, so the faerie will take this opportunity to trim the hair. They have a very small nose and their skin will be the colour of the flower they come from. They will have a strong aroma, the same as the flower family they were born into.

Flora faeries will always only ever have a relationship with a Flora faerie from the same flower, so a Bluebell Flora faerie will only have babies with another Bluebell Fauna faerie, a Daisy Flora faerie with a Daisy Flora faerie and so on. Their ears are the same shape as the flower they originate from, so if they are from a Bluebell they will have ears the same shape as Bluebell petals. Their wings are quite small, four in number, round edges for girls and pointed edges for boys. Each wing can move independently of each other and move very fast, leaving a kind of green glow around them when they are flying.

They are very hygienic and will use the streams to wash and drink from, hence, another reason why we as humans need to look after our streams and water supply much better than we do. They make small instruments out of reeds which they use for social gatherings where they will dance and sing. They tend to stay with their parents for five years which is the longest time span of all the faeries. They are a very happy group which shows with their aura as the colour is as bright as their flower.

The Flora faerie can sense earthquakes or extreme weather and will make all the animals aware of these natural disasters, so they have time to hide or take shelter. There are many different kinds of Flora faerie and they are responsible for the flowers and plants of the outer woodland, fields, hollows and vales that exist from countries as far north as Sweden, Russia, down to Italy and Greece, Japan and North America. The Flora faerie are known to gather in great numbers.

Flora faeries are very friendly with bees, when they gather pollen they make themselves invisible. They use a little sack made from plant fibres to collect the pollen in. They do depend a lot on honey for their energy, so you can see the lives of the bees are very important to both the Flora faeries and the flowers for without the bees, the faeries and flowers would struggle for survival. Can you imagine a world without bees, flowers or faeries? Pollution, insecticides and pesticides are not helping them! Already we see bees dying in great numbers. What can you do to change this?

If by any chance they happen to overeat, their faces will become rounder, their cheeks will sag and they become grumpy. They will stay this way until they have digested the food they ate too much of. If this happens they are told to pick up sticks until they work off the food they ate, this doesn't take too long and helps them remember what happens if they do eat too much.

The Flora faeries will use petals from the plant they are associated with for clothing and hats. You can tell which plant the Flora faeries are from by the way they dress. This could be the Daisy, Blackberry, Morning Glory, Gardenia, Snowdrop, Bluebells or Heather, the colour of the plant will also be reflected in the hair colour of the faeries. Their body is very similar to a human and they may wear simple clothing such as pants which reach down to their knees. They tend to wear shoes made from the wings that have been discarded by beetles and they will use small pieces of glass to trim their hair, clothing and shoes. They might even use horsehair to tie their shoes on by lacing them around their ankles.

Flora faeries may live underground in rabbit warrens or other small burrows which have been left empty, they will even sleep in hedgerows. Sometimes they may even share these burrows with the Assiseeas faeries in the next chapter. The Flora faeries have to sleep for two hours every eight hours or they become very tired. They have special relationships with mice, sometimes sleeping with them to keep warm. They sometimes ride on the backs of mice and moles. There is one peculiarity about the Flora faeries, that being they do not become stuck in spiders' webs. They just bounce off them and we are not sure how they do this. What do you think?

Chapter 5 - Assiseeas Faeries

The Assiseeas faeries are defined by their aura which is white and glows like a midnight star on a cold and frosty night. The Assiseeas can be anywhere in size between one half of an inch up to three inches, so they can be quite a small faerie. They inhabitat certain areas such as cliffs, mountain tops, rocky outcrops, colder places, and areas where rare plants might bloom and grow, such as heather and daisy flowers. They are a beautiful fine boned faerie and can be bright white or a shining black colour, either way they are very beautiful and colourful. It all depends on their heritage and the flower they came from. They could be short and round or taller and thin.

They have toes and fingers just like humans, their mouths are pink or yellow and their nose could be round or flat depending on the flower they come from. Their noses may be yellow or pink but their eyes are always a cornflower blue. The eyes have a pupil which is half the size of the eye, with a little bit of white in the far corner of the eye. The eye is elliptical in shape with eyelashes and eyelids which meet in the middle of the eye but they do not have eyebrows. Their ears are pointed at the bottom and top with the point always being at the back edge of the ear. Their hair is always the colour of the plant they originated from. Even ebony Assiseeas have hair the colour of the plant they are associated with, which makes them a very striking and beautiful faerie, as you can imagine. Their hair grows about half an inch a year and they will cut each other's hair by chewing it. Some they will eat and some they will keep for making baskets, hats or clothing as they do not like to waste anything.

The Assiseeas are associated with many flowers, most of which are in the wild including Buttercups. They are also responsible for flowers such as Sunflowers and ornamental gardens. Can you imagine how many faeries would be required to look after a Sunflower farm? They will live for about one hundred earth years after which they return to the spirit world. The remains of the faeries will be buried in the ground and in a very short time a new flower will grow from their remains. Interestingly, this flower will have the power of speech and will also have the memory of the faerie's previous life which is a shared memory with the actual faerie.

They have a glowing third eye crystal in their forehead which will be an iridescent blue, slightly deeper than their eyes. The Assiseeas have wings which are two thirds the size of their body, so a three inch faerie will have two inch wings. There are four wings which are pointed and grow from just between the shoulders and these wings can work independently of each other. The wings are very similar to Dragon Fly wings. The Assiseeas do have a Prima Assiseeas faerie who will guide them in completing their tasks for the day. You can tell which is the Prima faerie as it's third eye crystal will be brighter and have a purple aura to it. They will speak a form of Kreak, even though there are different dialects of Kreak, all the faeries will still somehow understand each other. A Prima Faerie are faeries that have learnt to give just that little bit more.

The Assiseeas will wash three or four times a day, perhaps whilst they are washing the clothing they are making, they will sing and their songs may remind you of a whale song. It might surprise you to learn that they love to take mud baths, as the mud may contain necessary minerals and salts to help keep their skin shiny. They are not confined to any particular area on earth and will live anywhere in the world where their flowers grow.

They tend to sleep almost any place, an old nest, in and around flowers and tending to doze off in the afternoons. Over their lifetime they may have two or three babies, usually mate

for life and have a kind of wedding ceremony called a 'Malacca'. At least once or twice a month they will have gatherings to sing and dance, perhaps using a leaf to make a sound like a flute. They might use horse hair tied between two plants which they will pluck to make a musical sound. They will sing about places they have lived and places that may have been destroyed by humans and how these areas once were before they were laid to waste.

They will use petals from the flowers to make a hat or clothing, if they breathe on the petals, the petals will not decay or wither as their breath contains a kind of preservative. They always make clothing for other faeries, giving them away and never keeping for themselves. They never think about expecting a gift in return, they just like to give things because they are able to do so. They normally wear a tunic on top with a kind of skirt on the bottom. They work very closely with the bees as the bees are so important to the pollination of the flowers. Without the bees, the flowers would not exist and in fact without bees, the whole of humanity and their way of life would be in jeopardy. Ask your teachers to explain why this is so?

The ebony Assiseeas will mainly look after roots of the flower and the ivory Assiseeas will look after the flower part of the plant, in essence you have two distinct types of Assiseeas faeries. Some ebony faeries may even have to dig up a plant and move it to a new location so that the flower can survive. The flowers always complain when this happens but they know it is in their best interest to be moved. At this present time, many flowers have to be moved due to pollution. What kind of pollution do you think affects a flower's health and ability to survive and grow?

Chapter 6 – Bell Faeries

Apart from belonging to the Bell flower family they also love to hear anything that sounds like a bell, raindrops splashing in puddles, (most especially), waterfalls, and even wind chimes in gardens. Bell faeries are related to the Flora and Sheharnie faeries. The Bell faeries have horizontal eyelids and almond shaped eyes the colour of their flower, unlike us humans who have vertical eyelids. The Bell flowers differ greatly in shape and colour, so you can imagine these faeries might look very different to each other. The shape of their head will reflect the shape of their Bell flower with their head having a slight point at the top.

Bell faeries are between three and five inches in height and there are both males and females. Their wings may look like what people consider faerie wings to be as they look very much like butterfly wings. The wings are the colour of their flower and are very beautiful. If you were to look at a Bell faerie from behind, you might think you were looking at a Bell flower. When the wings are open they are about twice the size of the faerie. You cannot tell the difference between male and female wings of a Bell faerie.

Their hair is very similar to our human hair and they arrange their hair just as we do. It is very rare for them to ever cut their hair and you may see them with hair down to their feet. Their nose looks similar to their plant, quite small but with a keen sense of smell. They are able to smell rain many miles away and become very excited when they know rain is coming. Their lips and eyes are the colour of their flower. Their hair will be the colour or colours of the flower's roots, so a Bluebell faerie will have white hair, blue eyes, blue wings and a green body stocking. Very colourful and very pretty, do you not you think? Their ears are round at the bottom and pointed at the top. They do wear shoes except when it rains, and will remove them so they can splash and dance in the puddles. If they are working in the rain, they may sometimes use their wings as an umbrella.

As with many faeries they will mate for life, but they will not always stay together all the time. With the Bell faeries, instead of blowing their breath into their hands to make a new baby Bell faerie, they will instead both blow their love breath into the closed bud of their flower. The female will always blow first, the new baby may take several days to form, but eventually the flower will open and out will pop a new baby Bell faerie. Is that not that something? The young faerie will stay around the parents for a long time.

Their aura is a glow of white light around them, as they become wiser their aura will become more intense in colour. The Bell faeries do not have a Prima faerie but they do have wiser faeries that are more experienced in the ways of giving. The Bell faeries could be considered part of the Flora Folk, as they are tied to a specific group of plants and flowers. These are the Bell flowers and hence they are called the Bell faerie. Their associated flowers could also be Bluebells, Hyacinths and Fuchsia.

These faeries are not restricted to any one area on earth, belonging anywhere you might find their flowers, but mostly in the cooler northern parts of the earth. They sleep and sing songs of raindrops. You might think it is raining in a wood but it could be the sound of the Bell faeries singing. They tend to sleep in the open, gathering around the plants or flowers, sometimes sleeping in holes left by other animals. They take many catnaps but like to sleep out of the wind in a warm area and feed on nectar from the plants.

They will wear hats sometimes made from the petals of their flower and will wear a kind

of body stocking from their ankles to their shoulders, which will be a green colour. This is made by weaving strands of the plants into a fine material and from this they make their clothing. They might also use yarn spun from caterpillars as the sticky substance holds the fibres together.

The Bell faeries have no natural enemies, are a very social group and never argue. Animals can see them and they will play with water droplets on spiders' webs or maybe ride on the backs of snails. They are responsible for protecting and helping their flowers to grow and prosper, especially in times of droughts or floods.

Chapter 7 – Pickit Dwarfs

As the name implies, this is exactly what the Pickit Dwarfs do, they pick up things and put them away. Pickit Dwarfs are descended from human beings that did not actually make it through the full term of pregnancy, for whatever reason that may be. When the spirit from the baby transcends back to the spirit world, they will have a chance to become a Pickit Dwarf, this can happen to any nationality or race on earth.

Pickit Dwarfs like to move things in peoples' homes, they like to do this just for fun, because they are still children, and like all children, they like to have fun! They never grow into a full adult, which is one of the reasons they are so well liked. They will have the looks of the child had they grown up as a human, except now they will never appear to get any older than the age of five, a little bit like Peter Pan you could say. They do have a fascination for the small things that humans leave lying around the home. They like to play games with humans that always like everything to be in it's place, just for fun. It could be their way of trying to tell them to not be so worried about everything being so perfect.

They are a very caring spirit and like to be around humans that are also very loving and caring, perhaps these humans might not have had any children of their own. They never grow more than eight inches in height. They will not always remain as a Pickit Dwarf, only as long as they have a wish to do so, this could be a short period or a longer time.

Humans might see them as a very small light, not much bigger than a pin head. They are able to move objects in the physical world because they are so closely related to humans. They cannot bear to be around situations of violence or anger and in these instances they will move away. Sometimes they can prove to be quite tough, as they will also pick up human emotions and give back to the human, to help them regain their calmness and find themselves. They will learn the language of the humans they are around the most. Eventually, the Pickit Dwarfs will return to meet their natural parents in the spirit world. One person could attract hundreds of Pickit Dwarfs. Pickit Dwarfs have been around as long as there have been humans. They do not fight, they do not quarrel, they communicate by thought, which is how they are able to work closely with human emotions and understand them.

Pickit Dwarfs cannot fly, but they do have the ability to disappear and reappear whenever they wish, sometimes this can be a problem as they are known to reappear at the wrong destination. They never need to sleep, they are never spiteful and are always looking for a way of giving, perhaps giving their energy to human children that are having a miserable life; something with magic, some kind of happiness. As we all know there are many children on earth that are having a dreadful life. They have very intense white auras and this is how you would see them, a bright white light. They are also known to work with other faeries in times of need, even though they may be quite a bit larger than some of the other faeries, but they are so gentle they never present a problem.

They do not need to eat but that is not to say they never do, as every child likes a piece of chocolate. They do gather in groups for school, so you see even for the Pickit Dwarfs in the spirit world there is no escape from school! Many times small human children will be able to see and talk to the Pickit Dwarf children. Often a single children or lonely children may be telling the truth when they say they have a small friend that comes to play with them.

Children do not suffer from racism and neither do the Pickit Dwarfs, they are always curious about the different colours of the children around them but this is just curiosity. Racism is not a word they ever have to worry about. If only humans could act the same way, do you not think so?

Pickit Dwarfs will wear clothing they feel comfortable in, this could be any style of clothing from any time period. The one thing about their clothing is that it will never have any square edges, all the edges will be rounded, as if to represent that things always come in full circles. The clothing will also consist of very soft materials and they are always dressed in some kind of clothing. The clothing is made from the energy of their own minds, this is materialized into a kind of material that sparkles with their energy.

Pickit Dwarfs most definitely interact with animals, mainly the ones that are defenseless. They will try to protect the smaller gentler animals by chasing away the animals that present a danger to them. They are a very shy group of beings, but they seem to live to be able to pick things up and put them away, as they are always doing this. The Pickit Dwarf do not grieve for people or things because they realize nothing is ever lost.

Chapter 8 – Lissarqu Faeries

Lissarqu faeries are derived from the forms of the snake, lizard, turtle or tortoise. It would seem that many people are afraid of these reptiles, although they do come from a very noble race indeed. They represent the lizard and snake in their spirit form and strangely enough they do have wings. They are approximately ten inches in height and have eyes with large green irises and a narrow vertical pupil. They wear old skins as clothing and this reaches up to their neck and becomes part of them. They are neither male nor female, but do have very strong emotions. They do become very sad when they see their earthbound counterparts being treated badly, especially those that are in boxes or very tiny cages with no openings in them.

Lissarqus will have very little hair and many times will wear a hat that is like an upside down funnel. Why, we are not really sure but maybe because it makes them happy. The hat will also be made of discarded skin. Because they have very pure thoughts, you would see little pink florescent orbs around their head, these orbs will become attached to the hat and will look like the morning dew has settled on their hats.

They do not look like humans but more like a cross between a turtle, snake or lizard. They do not need to eat. They are a very ancient race and exist on many different planets, all at a different stage of development, but all are a very noble and ancient creature. They have small holes on the side of their heads which are their ears. Because they may come from a tortoise or turtle, you may think they are slow moving but they are not, they can move and fly very quickly. They have soft lips and a smooth white skin on their face. It is as if you have taken all the snakes, lizards, turtles and tortoises and merged them all into one being. They have fingers and nails as they do like to climb trees. They may walk upright or on all fours. The temperature does not affect them, but they do like to take 'Lissarqu naps' in the sun.

Their wings are as long as their legs and they have a set of four wings, these are transparent and hang downwards when not in use. They do not have tails which means they do have a bottom of which they will use frequently to sit on. They like to sit in the V of a tree just thinking. They tend to talk in pictures, a type of telepathy by transmitting images to each other. They have a very different laugh, when they laugh it has a hiss in it, they do this by curling their tongue and turning it into a flute. Why not try to say a few sentences with a hiss in the words! They sing to each other and they sing to other animals. They do not have an aura and there are no baby Lissarqu, they just are. When they sing it can sound like a flute, a bat or even a human whistling. They are very enlightened beings which we must never forget. They live quite solitary lives although they do come together on occasions when it is necessary. They do mix with other faeries, holding meetings to resolve situations at times such as those affected by the environment and pollution.

They are often dressed in the apparel that appears to be the same as the skin of a snake or lizard when they have shed these skins. The Lissarqus use a secretion from under their arms to apply this skin to themselves, the skins then shrink to become a perfect skin tight fit. As there are so many skins available, you can imagine how dazzling and beautiful the Lissarqu must look like.

The Lissarqus will try to help lizards, turtles, tortoises and snakes on earth by encouraging them to use their instincts to survive. If a habitat has been damaged, the Lissarqus try to encourage the snakes and lizards to move to a new location. They will help them to find a new home to live in. They try to look like the animals they wish to help and other

animals very rarely see them. They will only visit reptiles on earth that are in healthy living conditions. Zoos used to be terrible places for them to live, nowadays many zoos have improved the living conditions for some reptiles, but here is something you can do, pester zoos to improve the size and quality of living conditions for all animals! Small animals are not always happy in small cages. You can always complain to the zoos by sending them a letter. Have your parents or teachers help you do this.

Chapter 9 – Orchid Faeries – Members of the Whittle Group

The Orchid Faeries look very much like the plant they come from, this is more so than normal due to the fact that orchids have been around for such a long time. Orchid faeries will look very different from each other because the flowers themselves have so much variety in them. Their skin tone and colour may well alter and they will always have hair that has a mind all of it's own. Of course, any hair that has a mind of it's own will influence the colours of the hair and the faerie.

The skin of the faeries will reflect the colour of the green part of the flower, this could be a mossy green or a milky complexion. The faeries are very small, reaching only three inches maximum in height. Their feet will be green, as the green reaches up towards their shoulders, the green will change into small patterns of leaves. They have very thin arms, legs and bodies and they are very delicate in shape like the orchid flower itself.

Their nose will be in perfect proportion to the rest of their face, but will be shaped like the seed of the flower. Their eyes are a clear blue with no iris and no white and can be a powder blue to the deepest blue. They have eyelashes but no eyebrows. They tend to fly as quick as a hummingbird, fast and nimble. Their ears could be pointed or round and their hairline is pointed at the front. They have one set of wings, these wings have a small tail on the bottom of them. The tail itself has a small pattern on it that looks like an eye, similar to the patterns on some butterfly. The wings are pointed and clear and when it is raining they may fold the wings over their head. They cannot fly in the rain. Their wings will only appear after one year so in this time they become very good climbers.

The faeries love to balance on anything, particularly on branches in trees or where orchids may grow. They love to balance on one toe for hours, trying to look like an orchid flower. They do have a Prima faerie and they have a Prima for each type of orchid flower. There is also one Prima faerie that looks after all the Orchid faeries. The Prima faerie will have a jewel in it's forehead which is something it has to work very hard to create as it is the ability to give that creates this jewel. It is shaped like a teardrop, the colour is indigo with a pure white centre and the white can only be seen shining in the dark. The Prima faerie does not have a partner or have children.

Again, their hair has a mind all of it's own and this hair will be the colour of the orchid flower. If the hair agrees, the faerie will tie the hair back into a pony tail, however, many times the hair will not agree with the wishes of the faerie. The shape of the flower will always be reflected in the shape of the faerie, for instance long petals will result in long arms. Their lips are normally the colour of the stamen, this could be red, yellow or blue. As you can imagine the Orchid faerie will be very colourful. Their hair tends to be up to five times thicker than the other faeries and because of this, it can become messy or unruly, doing as the hair wishes. It is easy to imagine them having a bad hair day. Over the centuries, disagreements with their hair has become a little more diplomatic and washing and playing with their hair keeps the hair happy.

They are born the same way as the Whittle faerie, after blowing their breath into a flower a baby faerie will emerge after only eight hours, fully formed. Parents will have a maximum of four children in their lifetime, and these faeries live up to one hundred and twenty years on earth. Babies are always born on a midsummer's eve.

They will dance and sing like birds, mimicking the sounds of other creatures. The purpose of their gatherings will be to learn from each other and help each other. Their aura will vary from pink to white, depending on how active or healthy they are. Their shape is very similar to humans, they do not always wear clothing, as the green skin looks and acts like clothing. Their skin protects them from the rain and mist. On special occasions, Edwin the Dwarf will make simple clothing for them. The faeries come from all types of Orchid flowers, wherever they may grow. As with the flowers, the Orchid faeries give off a beautiful fragrance and they will always sleep in or around their flowers, wherever they may be. Wherever the Orchids grow so will the faeries be with them. This could be in forests or on the face of cliffs. Edwin the Dwarf will sometimes make a porcupine quill comb for the faeries to use to comb their hair.

They do have partners, normally this partnership lasts whilst they are on earth caring for the flowers. They help to convince the flowers to change as required, due to the climate changing. These faeries are also the principal keepers of the door to the faerie world, these doors are never in the same place. If a non-faerie being wishes to see the faerie world, it will be the Orchid faerie that organizes the event. They will also prepare the soil for new Orchids to grow, sometimes bringing water in a leaf to the flowers that do not directly receive enough rain. Because of the humans' complete disregard for the environment, the Orchid faerie try not to think of humans anymore, such a shame really as at one time, humans and faeries were visible to each other. What a world we have become, do you not you think?

Chapter 10 – Poppopolly Faeries

Poppopolly are a migrating faerie, drifting from one place to another, all depending on where they are needed most. For a large part of the year they are dormant, living mostly in the spirit world. The only time they will appear on earth is when their food is readily available. Poppopolly are a form of Flora faerie, they are associated most closely with one particular flowering form and that being the Poppy.

They do not seem to have the same fascination with physical life that other faeries have and their presence is not required for things to grow or to be motivated to grow. It isn't that they are selfish, quite the opposite is the case, but they do have a limited response to situations on our side of life. I suppose you could say they keep very much to themselves. They are in fact responsible for helping insects and other small creatures that have not yet discovered their real purpose in life. It is as if they are the Shepard's of the less intelligent creatures and because of this they are so readily accepted.

They are quite unusual for faeries, as it is not because of their size, they are only two and three quarter inches in height, but it is to do with the very fact that they have body hair. This body hair is very fine, though it is slightly longer than you would imagine. The body hair tends to be not overly obvious at first glance, they do not shave or pluck it as they quite like it. It gives them a furry appearance, as though they almost have a kind of halo all the way around them when you first see one. In relation to the skin itself, the hair stands off from the skin a full one eighth of an inch, which is actually a lot considering their small size. They have hair on their heads as well as their bodies, the hair on their heads is not more than a quarter inch long and never appears to grow. The Poppopolly have twenty to thirty hairs that are longer with sort of hooks on them on the front of it's torso. When sleeping the faerie curls up around the bottom of the stem of a poppy using these hairs to hold itself to the stem.

The infant Poppopolly will take several weeks for their wings to appear. The wings of a Poppopolly are very similar to a Butterfly and will actually be the same colour as the Poppy of which the faerie come from. The colour will not be just within the veins but the whole wing. The skin tone of a Poppopolly will usually be stark white, as though they have seen a ghost, or maybe like bone china or ceramic that miniature pictures are painted upon. Their skin texture is very fine and milky, the hair upon them looks once again like a halo effect or a very distinct pale aura but it is really just hair. In fact, their aura is yellow, but it tends to be quite a faint yellow. The colour of the hair on their body is very pale with a powder green tip to the hair. It is not really green, it is more white than green. It has just a mere hint of green and also a touch of yellow as well. The hair on the body is not as thick as the hair on their head, although it is very soft and downy and does stand out from the skin.

At the time when their love for each other has come to the extent that their hair recedes, only then will they go and find a particular flower with the purpose of bringing about a baby faerie to be born. What they will do is they will go in search of a suitable flower and older children will go looking for a flower as well. Sometimes they may not agree on a suitable flower and it may take several days to resolve the dispute. It is usually something to do with the actual location, whether they are going to get enough sun, as the sun is the ripening empowerment of the Poppopolly. You may well be aware that Poppies lose their petals very quickly through lack of sun or wind so the Poppopolly faeries actually choose very well the flower that they need. When they find a flower they agree on and whilst the poppy is still in bud, they will simply come upon it and the female will put her mouth immediately upon the flower on the end of the closed

bud and push her breath into the flower, quickly followed by the male faerie. That really is the only time that the male and female Poppopolly will mate, they will then disperse and possibly never see each other again, as they do not mate for life as it is with many other form of faeries.

A Poppopolly faerie in the spirit world is a small mass of energy that is a being, that is spirit. When Poppopolly wish to have a physical existence on earth and the breath is brought together by the parents, the cells within their breath join together. The faerie spirit in the spirit world will also be at the location of the flower waiting for the breath to be joined. It is the love between the two faeries that draws the faerie spirit to it. As the two cells meet, the spirit faerie seals the two cells together. At this moment when the cellular field is sealed in a kind of bubble of a semi-viscous fluid, this bubble grows and helps to maintain the cells within it, until in just a few days you will have a fully formed infant Poppopolly. At this stage of it's development, the Poppopolly will reflect the colours of the inside of the poppy of which it is lying, and very gradually these colours will become more pronounced and milkier as the Poppopolly takes shape.

The head and arms form as buds to begin with, and gradually it unfolds. It is as though it starts as a small ball and then gradually unfolds into the faerie being it is. The process takes just over a few days, really quite quick for a being to come into form. The wings will develop within a matter of weeks. The infant will spend most of these first few weeks close to the flower of it's surrogate parent, climbing up and down the stems and will be on the ground a lot of the time. They have small faces and small eyes, their eyes are perfectly round and completely black, they do not have any colour or white in their eyes. They do have one eyelid, which is at the top and moves up and down. One aspect with a Poppopolly is that you can not tell where it is looking unless it's head moves. They have a nose which is a little bit piggy, it has a flat piece at the end of it, which is from the top lip and is like a small disc. It is as if you have a small coin and you set it at an angle, perhaps sixty degrees from horizontal, and this forms the top lip. There are two small holes at the bottom of this.

Their mouth is small but defined with orange lips. They do not really have teeth but a form of tissue that calcifies and becomes quite hard. Teeth are not really required because they only really sip nectar. They do smile, their tongues are quite short but can be extended quite a ways. The tongue and inside the mouth is pink, more pink than humans, quite a dusty pink, a carnation pink. Their neck is short, they have four fingers and a thumb which is backwards, the thumb only comes into use when they are climbing the stem of a plant. Their nails do not really grow, they are really just hard pads that only become harder after several years.

They have ears which are almost round except that they go to a point at the back in the middle. If you were looking at the ear, the hole is to the front of the ear. It looks as if the ear has two flaps with one fitting inside the other. They can sometimes extend the flap more forward if they are listening to something, as the ear is able to move. The ear is smaller than a human in proportion to the head and their arms and legs are one third of their body height.

You can tell a male and female apart by the two red lobes which appear at the back of the neck, this is really the only way. There are no other visual signs which mark the difference in sex. The lobes are two small flaps that appear at the back of the neck where the neck joins the body. It is as if they have two false wing stubs and they are like two small buds. They are called lobes because they are flaps of skin that appear like ear lobes. The female has these while the male does not. The faerie is only active on earth when Poppies are available, the rest of the time they stay within the faerie world as they do not mix very well with other faeries. Within their two and three quarter inches of height, they have a body very similar to a human being, but they are not specifically tied to human beings as they are a separate species altogether. Poppopolly faeries have existed for thousands and thousands of years.

A band of Poppopolly faeries may be sixty to one hundred in number, sometimes more depending on how the faeries are attracted to a particular area. As soon as they began interacting with physical life, they found that the flower that created most joy in their heart was the various varieties of Poppy. Red Poppy, Giant Poppy, California Poppy, all are of course quite different to one another. Other Poppies include a selection of ones like Day Poppies which only last very, very briefly and have gentler colours. They were attracted specifically because of their petals, they feel the petals are something they can wrap themselves in. They are attracted to the colour because of its vibrancy, even with the paler poppies. They really are very attracted to colour, it always makes them happy. They tend to wash in rainwater, and rainwater only, if there has been no rain they will go and find some. At times if there is no rain they will go in search of a cloud and wash in that. They very rarely come into homes, but they are known to be in gardens, particularly those with many flowers.

When it comes to their clothing, there is a particular form of Dwarf who help in this regard, making clothing for them on their behalf. These are special clothes which once they are given to the faerie and the faerie puts them on, then clothes become a part of the faerie, like a second skin. This is because the clothes have the same cellular memory and appearance as the faerie itself. This may be difficult for human beings to understand but this is because humans are not unified with the clothes they wear. Faerie on the other hand are extremely excited by the clothes they wear, particularly if they have been made for them by someone else. These clothes are very refined, they tend to be made from Poppy petals which are torn into very thin strands and woven together to form a kind of cloth. This is then treated with a special liquid, the recipe of which is only known to the Dwarfs who make them. The Dwarfs make these in the faerie world and then they bring them once they are finished. They usually make four or five pieces of clothing at a time for the particular faerie who need them. They do not wear jewelry, but they will occasionally wear a small hat, this is a small round hat which they make themselves. This just fits on the top of their heads and is made out of the Poppy petal. They just pull the petal apart so that it fits, this is the only form of decoration they ever use.

They play with snails all the time and is the only time they will ever play with other beings. What they do is gently grab their eyes, because if you remember a snail's eyes are on stalks. They grab the eye stalks from behind and hold on for a ride, although a very slow ride. Even though snails eat poppies, it does not mean this will be the end of the plant, many plants that they eat may have already seeded. There will always be some who have managed to seed so that plants will still be able to grow and the spirit of that poppy will still move on and on. Otherwise, these faeries have a very limited connection with animals, mice can see them and they appear to be the only animal they interact with apart from the snails.

They will live for about fifty earth years and during which time they can appear and disappear at will. Where they go nobody knows!

Chapter 11 – Sariisia Faeries

The Sariisia faeries are between three and five inches in height. They have a human like form including a male and female Sariisia, with the females having hair very much like humans. Sariisia are in fact related to humans, but in a different way than you may think. Long, long ago, at a time when humans were less materialistic, and more informed and inviting of the faerie world, they were actually friendly with Sariisia. The Sariisia became a kind of 'go between', as they were very conciliatory, making good ambassadors and still are.

The actual contact between human form and Sariisia came from some forms of the human fetus that for whatever reason did not make it past two to four months. This spirit is then given the chance to become a faerie but that was many, many thousands of years ago. However, when there became a breakdown in the relationship between Sariisia and humans, this option of becoming a faerie stopped being possible. This small band of Sariisia then began reproducing themselves through the normal faerie method of transferring their breath, which is a form of transferring cells from one to another and mixing them up. They will first use an Iris or a Flag flower that denotes their genetics and their family. The female would blow her breath into the Flag flower and very carefully close it with it's hands, and then open it again very carefully, the male Sariisia would also do the same. It would take perhaps four days for the new Sariisia faerie to emerge, during which time the female Sariisia, as it is only the female that can secrete the gooey substance from their mouths, will glue the flower shut.

They do have a great similarity to humans, not one specific type, or race, they may have the form of several races. The form of facial expressions or facial features will be determined by the genetic history and the family history of the particular group. It will also be determined by the specific flower that they come from. They will have arms, legs and a body which is in proportion to the rest of it, as you would expect a small thin human being to be. They are quite alive and they never over eat. You will never see an overweight Sariisia faerie, as this is because it has a very quick metabolism. They will exist within physical life for somewhere between seventy or eighty years. This is very similar to a human, although they do not age as humans do, so they are very lucky in this respect. Over time their hair will gradually turn white, even if their hair started black when they were born.

Their hair colouring will reflect the actual centre of the plant flower they were born in. Many Irisis and Flags will have different colour petals, perhaps showing two or three tones within their actual petal colour. It may be with certain forms of Flag flowers that the petals have very deep colours, perhaps deep purple and deep reds. They may have a velvety feel and touch to them and their hair will reflect whatever colour the central darker element of the flower is. So you can imagine then perhaps, that as the faeries continue through their cycle that this colour will gradually lighten after a period of about forty years. The changing of the hair colour is really the only sign of any form of the aging process.

Sariisia faeries will have five fingers including the thumb along with five toes on each hand and foot. Their arms have a wrist, an elbow and a shoulder joint, and there are hips, knees and ankles. They have two sets of wings which work independently of each other. One set of wings will work in one direction and the other may work in a different direction. Their wings are very similar to Dragon Fly wings.

With the Sariisia faeries that come from a Flag flower they will look similar to the flower, but with a pale interior with streaks becoming darker to the outer edges of the flower. This is how the body colour of the Sariisia will look. These streaks of colour will come from the feet all the way up the Sariisia themselves. These streaks will not deviate and they will be straight up the body and will cease or come to an end at the shoulder.

Whatever is the lightest colour of the flower will be the colour of the skin of the Sariisia including the face. Although, if the genetics of the Sariisia come from a fetus with parents from Africa you may well have a face with the skin colour from the people of that particular continent on earth. The hair will reflect the darker colour of the flower. They have green eyes and their irises are like those of a cat, with the slits downwards which are black, this does not normally expand outwards unless they are singing. When they sing the pupil becomes fixed and dilated, and they do love to sing. There is no white in the eye, only a murky transparency that you cannot see through. Their eye shape is quite round, there is an eyelid which has hair for the eyelash, the same colour as the hair on their head which has a top and a bottom eyelash. It is only the top eyelid that comes down as they have a very faint line of hair for the eyebrow, but they are not really eyebrows in human terms. This runs further down the sides of the head than in humans, so when it rains, the rain is directed away from their eyes and down the sides of their faces instead.

Their ears will have small points only on the upper edge, with the point leaning slightly to the rear of the edge of the ear. Their ears are similar in proportion to human ears, if anything a little smaller. They have voices which means they have a voice box and is a part of the genetic history of their family orientation. Their nose tends to be quite small, not pronounced in any way and quite perfectly formed. It is a kind of button nose, although the nostrils themselves will be a little more wider placed than you would expect. The lips are quite pronounced for a faerie, and they will be in the staple colour of the faerie between light and dark.

They do have an aura, which surrounds the faeries and becomes more evident as their age progresses. The aura colour itself is between blue and green, is quite faint, but will be seen quite clear, particularly at dusk and is the blue of a lake and green of newborn oak. Their tongue is typically the colour of the stamen of the flower, it may be bright yellow or another colour. Rather than having nails they will instead have pads which is different to many other faeries.

They are very good swimmers but do not have gills because they are able to transform oxygen. The fish do not eat them merely because they are so quick and such good swimmers, using their bottom pair of wings as propellers. The top pair of wings are folded up when they are swimming and they fold them up lengthways. So if you can imagine Dragonfly wings, the Sariisia are able to close the wings so they become a thin pencil or a reed which is then laid down the back.

During their lifetime on earth they may have between three to seven offspring which will entirely depend upon how many different relationships they have. If they have long, deep relationships and are closely harmonic they will continue it and will perhaps have four or five offsprings, as is usually the case for Sariisia faeries. The family may be together for a long time, it can be many seasons or many years. It may be for some, that they are together throughout their entire existence whilst in a physical state. The Sariisia exist in groups, as the flowers can be in groups of five or tens or hundreds. It all depends on the place and the area where they reside. They are very good healers and can bring the ease of suffering to many different forms of life, just by their presence.

They are principally associated with Flags, Irises, Water Irises and also those that grow upon the land, in marshy areas or just in gardens. They will sleep in an Iris clump, or a Flag clump or wherever it is that the plant happens to be; frequenting places like large reed beds as well as in the water margins of predominantly fresh water. Sometimes they are at the land where it meets the shore of a stream or river but it will always be where Reed Flags or other forms of Iris type plant are in abundance. They are considered a summer faerie as during the long winter months they will be asleep. They may come into homes if there are flowers of their origin, they will visit them as the flowers will call to them, even cut flowers. This is anywhere on earth where these flowers exist. As the flowers bloom at different times all over earth, the Sariisia faeries will move to those areas, including the areas where these flowers are mass produced and cut for resale.

Their clothes are made out of reeds, or the petals of the flower itself which they coat in a kind of sticky goo that they are able to produce in their mouths, which they put in their hands and rub all over the surface. They will perhaps use one petal split in half with one for each legging being pulled on like tubes. They will very often use Iris and Flag petals for a kind of flowing tubing with both genders doing this. They do not bother cutting them into a specific shape, rather letting the flower itself depict how it feels. When they have done with it, or if it breaks, they just merely throw it away and make another. When it comes to making clothing for the body, they will merely cut or bite a hole in the back where the wings are attached. Due to the short lifespan of their flowers they may occasionally run out of petals. If this happens they always have petals that have been preserved with a goo and saved for the time when there is a shortage. The longer the goo stays on the clothing, the stronger it becomes. All of the artistry for making the clothes will have to be done quite quickly before the goo sets. The females will make clothes for the males and it is the one activity that they actually do interacting with one another. It is not that they do not do anything for anyone else, as they do, as they are very inter-social. They don't usually wear shoes, they may at times weave small intricate bracelets which become gifts from one to another, it is to define their relationship.

They do interact with insects and animals. When they are in the spirit world they still remain as ambassadors. This is where they continue their stewardship if you like, and is their way of being able to communicate between other species. They are very good healers, they bring the ease of suffering to many different forms of life just by their presence.

Chapter 12 – Tree People

Trees are ordinarily very well behaved, and so too are the Tree People. In fact they are peaceful and completely at peace with who they are. The Tree People occupy a great difference in size and length. Their appearance can be most odd, so they will not necessarily have a human like form at all. They may well have a form that is depicted by the species of tree of which they are a part of.

So how to describe a Tree being? Well, we shall have to take one as an example! How about an Evergreen tree, perhaps a Douglas Fir or something like that, maybe that would be appropriate to begin with. A Tree being from the species of Douglas Fir as it is called in human terms, is not called Douglas or Fir! The Tree People have different names that were given to them by their ancestry. Their appearance then tends to be that of a head which is very similar to the cone that the Fir produces. It is marbled in texture and round which goes to a point at the top. So you could say, it is a little bit like a pear drop or a teardrop shaped head. The Tree being itself does not come into life in the physical sense, the same way as other faerie do. It is not a physical thing that occurs, but it is that they draw their essence from the trees of which they are a part of. They come straight from the ether world, or what you could also call the spirit world. I suppose in many respects, that is why some faeries or some human beings in fact do feel that the Tree People are faeries, because they are materialized spirits that are attached to a particular species of tree and who adorn themselves with the physical elements of likeness of the tree itself.

Their fingers may well be like needles, if we are referring to the Douglas Fir and those who belong to them. As well as a head like a raindrop, they have slanted eyes which are set at a forty five degree angle in the front of their head. And yes, they even have two holes which are the nose and a small bump where the nose would normally be. They have a mouth with sharp jagged teeth, yet they do not actually use them to eat anything as they materialize fully formed. The Tree Peoples' fingers may well be of a needle like quality. They tend to move themselves with extreme dexterity, and are very delicate beings generally. They have a chameleon like appearance in the way of their movement and they are very careful about where they stand or where they sit.

They can change their size from just a few inches to eight or nine feet, they may even change themselves into a seedling, and mimic the structure of a young tree of the species it belongs to. For the most part they will stay in the neighborhood of their own trees. But what happens if a human cuts a tree down, or if it falls down, or if something else is wrong with it? What will happen is, it will simply use it's mind thought to disappear. It will gather all of it's cellular memory and visit somewhere else. They do mourn every single tree that dies, but they do not remain mournful. They move on because there is the very heavy business of making sure that all of the other trees of the same type and form are well and looked after.

Trees themselves have a very strange thought form, as you can well imagine. They may sigh, they may have feelings, particularly if they become diseased or if they are attacked by some wild fungus, or if they have some of their limbs amputated unnecessarily so, just because people do not like their shape. When trees feel at peace they bring the ambience of their peaceful state to the rest of the area in which they live. You can feel when a tree is vibrant and happy because it has a very bright aura and some humans can even see it. Alternatively then if it is very unhappy, it will be disheveled and shriveled. It will not be as bright or uplifting, it will lose its luster, it will even slow it's growth to almost nothing and it can be sad. It does not

really have a very specific language structure, but it shares feelings with other trees.

When you trim a tree for whatever reason, they do mourn themselves just like carrots, but that is not to say you cannot eat the carrots! It is only a temporary thing. When we trim trees they do understand why we are doing so. If a diseased limb is removed they understand it is for the right reason and are actually quite relieved when it is dealt with because this means it cannot infect the rest of the tree. In this case, the Tree People have to communicate with them and that is why they are there. It actually helps if you are to do some work upon a tree, that you ask them first, that you tell them what you are going to do and why. You ask for their forgiveness if they should feel affronted at this attack and that you do so with the best intentions. They do not understand our language but what they do pick up on is our sensitivity and the empathy that we bring across to them. When we bring our feelings and what we are trying to put across, they understand, as the Tree People can read thoughts.

They will sometimes sit upon the stumps or stand upon them. They have legs and feet, but their legs do not bend, their feet are claw like and that enables them to climb. They do not climb very often because they usually just float up and down. They use their feet and limbs if they have any, to hang on to wherever it is they have arrived at on the tree. They do not have knees in their limbs, their limbs are just straight, sometimes their limbs may even blend into one with their foot. Their feet are more like roots, very short roots. They tend to use their roots and branches to move up the bark of the tree. Oak beings do not float, it is usually the evergreen variety that float. The Oak beings' eyes are elliptical but set in a vertical way. The eyes are black with no colour, they have eyelids that are sharp, or they can be sharp. The eyes or eyelids are protected by a bark like structure which may or may not be present upon the surface of the acorn face.

An Oak tree person would have an acorn shaped head with the cap that the acorn grows into forming a hat upon it's head. They most certainly do not have hair, either self-thinking or otherwise. They don't have skin but they do have bark which you could say is a kind of skin. It will have the body of the bark, which is a kind of slate grey in colour and somewhat knobbly. It's arms will have bends in them that are permanent, and the bends will not necessarily be in one particular direction. It could have two to four arms, with twig like fingers that have leaves upon them that can bend to the will of the tree being. This particular tree is deciduous in real life so in winter the Tree being will blend in to the form of the tree, and they will leave that form there, perhaps the spirit will leave it there completely for the duration of the winter. The form just merely sleeps as a part of the bark. It will lose it's leaves, which are formed as fingers on the very end of the twig.

The Tree People are not allocated a specific tree, they go where they wish. There may be three or four Tree people at one tree at any one time. A tree will know well in advance when it is to pass, because it can feel it. They have knowledge of when their time is coming to an end. They will tend to migrate when the last seeds have left, going with them to a new place. The trees do not necessarily pass to the spirit world, they will leave the husk of what the tree was at a convenient time close to when the physical tree itself is going to pass. That is why mourning by the Tree People is so short because the Tree beings in this sense, the tree spirit of the pure physical tree will actually migrate to a new place in the physical world in the form of a seedling. It does not die or have a new life, it is merely continuing the life it had in a new form. In that respect you would have a species of tree which is very ancient and which has always existed. In a sense, the tree that you are talking with or perhaps communicating with is a form of a seedling. It does not die or have a new life, it is merely continuing the life it had in a new form. In that respect you would have a species of tree which is very ancient and which has always existed. In a sense the tree that you are talking with or perhaps communicating with on our side of life, may appear only to be fifty or eighty years old, and yet really it's spirit is of an ancient destiny.

They do not have predators because they are not physical. Even when they manifest in the physical they do not need to be protected by anything. They do not get eaten by bugs because the bugs do not find them very tasty. Termites do not worry them either, nor woodlice, beetles or any other insects. An indication of the Tree Peoples' presence is the feeling of their aura. If they are surprised at all they will simply put their roots into the ground and become a sapling with leaves or whatever is expected for that time of year. They do send calls to other faeries if they need their aid in something they cannot help or manifest themselves. Their main function is really about the ambiance and quiet stillness of the environment that they create, or that they help to create by their presence. Their presence helps make the other trees, even if they are not of that species, feel secure.

There are not any trees that do not have Tree faeries. It would be one type of Tree faerie that represents a species of tree, not a faerie for every type of tree within that species of tree. Whether it is one that has thorns or one that does not, it may be of course that you may have both, and that they both belong to the same species. This means there are many types of Tree faeries. For example, some May Tree are very thorny and as such may form differently. Even May Trees may appear in slightly different forms or shades and the Tree People from this species will appear different, accordingly.

At Christmas time, trees are much happier to be left to grow to a fully grown Christmas tree. It is the hope of all young trees that are to become Christmas trees that perhaps they will be forgotten and they will be allowed to grow into full mature trees. The Tree People do visit tree farms, surveying them, trying to put them at ease. Christmas trees do know they will only have a short life. It is one of the reasons why it is so much kinder to have them growing in a pot rather than chopping them down, or maybe even consider buying a fake one!

Tree People may look exactly the same as a young seedling for a while or, they may become a part of a major tree which has grown for one hundred or over two hundred years. They will form themselves in these ways to maintain the link between themselves and the tree of which they are a part. The Tree People when they wish to move from one forest to another, merely vanish and arrive at the place they had thought of. Thought is created to an animated mind, the animated mind exists in the spirit world and they are able to make contact in an instant. Decisions are made through the advantage of being able to look at self beyond self at the same moment. They may observe the situation surrounding them from a different perspective or of a different dimension.

When Tree People wish to move in a physical way, they will glide using the aerodynamic forces of changing their molecular structure to the weight of air, so that when they decide that they want to be somewhere else, they can be. Perhaps it may be that they actually wish to climb the tree or something like that, they will wait for a convenient breeze and merely change their molecular structure into the weight of a feather. It will still have the same appearance, but it will merely mean that it will be virtually weightless.

They only work at night, during the day they become part of their native genetic tree. They are still there but they will have blended into the tree. Sometimes they will actually change their shape slightly so that their blending is more proficient, and more exact. They will squeeze themselves very thinly and stand up very straight and tall so that they become part of the bark. The Tree People tend to visit places usually at night, they will just appear and be with those of their kin that they are familiar with. They do not have elbows, they have limbs that are very similar to tree limbs.

Contrary to popular belief they are not sullen, they are actually very happy beings because trees themselves produce so much good for the earth. It is not trees that produce large quantities of methane, it is the animals that live upon them and around them that create the methane gas. Trees themselves by night create carbon dioxide, as do all plants, which is why hospitals take plants out of rooms at night. By day they bring forward the taking in of carbon dioxide and exuding of oxygen, which they produce in far greater abundance than any other gas in their exchange of life. It is quite wrong to say that trees themselves create harmful gases for the planet upon which you live. They are most beneficial, you only have to walk into a forest, particularly a rain forest in order to appreciate the grand variety and the microbiology that they exude of their own standing. However, in the rain forests it is quite stressful for the trees, since they know what is coming, they are trying to produce more seeds so that they may leave that place, or that the seeds may be buried for some time in the future to be able to germinate, re-grow and replace what was lost.

The Tree People do not only observe or look after the rights of their particular species or group, but it is within their own individual species that they will feel most at home, and in fact will be the very place where they will be able to form as though a part of the living tree itself. The Tree People communicate with those they represent in the vegetable kingdom, trees are in fact the largest of organisms that may live on our side of life. Trees as beings appear on the surface to be silent, and so the Tree People are their voice and they are responsible for their well-being. When they are working, they communicate with the tree on which they are servicing at that time. They instruct the tree on perhaps how to drop it's seeds or which wind it should wait for in order to let them go. They will see if there are any things that they need, such as other minerals or salts that may be left lying around. They sometimes liaise with other faeries to bring things to them to help the tree to grow in a better way.

They are a very ancient people because Tree people began at a time when there were strange animals on our side of life. They came and went as the different forests changed and altered their course. The Tree People actually share in their responsibility along with other faerie folk of dispersing seeds from respective trees. It is not something that is just down to climate or the weather, it is something that they actively pursue. Perhaps, they may after some catastrophic event, help plant the various seeds from plants that have burst open, for example from a forest fire or something like that. This is how they preserve the genetic structure and the spirit from one tree to another as they walk across the landscape of our side of life.

Chapter 13 – Trumpetears Faeries

Trumpetears are known for their shyness, they will hide, sometimes even within a flower itself as they are able to shrink at will and make themselves smaller to the point of invisibility. They are not wholly physical at all, in fact they are really a true representation of the spirit world in a physical form, temporarily exposed.

Trumpetears are usually of a glossy green body type that includes their fingers, their arms all the way up to their shoulders. They have arms and legs exactly the same as human beings. Where the green meets their shoulders they exhibit the same colour as the flower from which they are born and a part of. One of the main attractions of Trumpetears are their scent as they are the aromatic faerie. They are long and thin, growing to a maximum height of four inches, though generally they are seen as being around two inches. A Trumpetears main attraction, I suppose you could say is their ears, because their ears are like trumpets, which is why they have their name Trumpetears. Their ears are almost the length of their head and they hang down as a small tube with a flared end, the ears have their own will, and can actually strain and change direction when they want to.

The ears have small green veins upon them, which the Trumpetears have running up their neck and all over its head to the crown. These tiny, minutest veins are green, as green as the green of the actual body, legs, arms, hands and fingers itself. These veins run throughout the body's surface. They do not wear anything on their feet and have four toes and four fingers. They have a thumb which is unlike a human thumb as it comes from the centre of the wrist which is quite flexible as the wrist can actually move a whole three hundred and sixty degrees on it's own axis. Trumpetears have extremely attentive minds, they are able to diminish themselves with their own thoughts. It is in fact how they disappear from human sight or from the sight of anything they do not wish to be viewed by.

They have wings as well, so you can see there is no surprising one because they have all situations and areas completely covered. They are able to fly at extreme speed or velocity from a standing start. Their wings are quite long and thin and are typically three quarters of their total height, they are fixed at one end at the shoulder with the tips of the wings down towards the floor. So their wings do not sit up above their heads, like flies I suppose you could say. They are quite long and thin and they do not have a second pair. The wings have very thin green veins, dark green veins which are surrounding the pockets of a minutely thin membrane, so very similar I suppose to a fly's wing in that respect.

Their faces are round, almost perfectly round, each one's face will depend upon the colour of the plant of which they are born as there will be some genetic reference to that plant. They have hair, in particular they have three threads that are at the front and make up a peak, these three threads are somewhat longer and thicker than the rest of the hair which is short. The head of hair is generally quite short, not because they keep it cut but because it does not grow. The hair is very slow growing and they will produce a tiny bud upon the end of each strand of hair.

The bud itself will be the same colour as the bud of the flower from which they hail. The colour of the hair itself tends to be a similar colour to the branches of whatever their plant happens to be. Now understand, that generally due to the different plant varieties and because of the fact that they are evergreen, their branches tend to be quite dark and that the hair is dark green in colour. The buds of course never open but they are there really to denote that

the faerie itself is capable of reproducing.

They do not have eyebrows but do they have almond shaped eyes which have a point to the outer edge, so they are more elliptical towards the middle of the face and toward the outer edge they are more pointed. They have eyelids which close from the top to the bottom and eyelashes which actually bend downward not upward, this is because although their cheeks are fairly small they are actually quite rounded and so when the eyelid closes the eyelash rests upon the rounded cheek. Do not forget the eye is quite large and so the eyelashes will be quite long. The eyelashes are there as a form of protection.

They also have a third eye, but this does not grow for many years, as you may well recognize by now there is actually a Prima Trumpetears. The third eye itself will not become evident until the Trumpetears are at least forty earth years of age. It's aura begins to manifest itself in a very faint powder blue, it will grow and alter and gradually change depending upon the abilities of the Trumpetears to maintain it's giving possibilities. It will change in brightness and it will change in density, not just in the luminosity of it but also it will actually become deeper as though looking into it you would see other colours within. Similar perhaps to the past history of the genetics of the plant itself.

The nose has two trills, it has two small holes at the bottom and has quite a round end to a fairly short but thin nose. The nose has a round bulbous little end to it, which is always a bright red. In fact the more mature and the more giving the faerie becomes the brighter red the nose becomes. As you can imagine the Trumpetear is quite a striking faerie. Their lips are thin and blue, very thin in fact like a small pencil line. They have teeth and drink water and honey, they do not eat but drink it. They lap it up through their long thin pink tongue which has a squared end to it. They have yellow nails which many faerie do not. They have long thin arms and legs with knees which are backwards so they are backwardly facing knees.

They have names which are peculiar to them and speak Kreak as do most faeries. They do wash and usually in rainwater or crystal spring water. They do like to bathe quite a lot, so they will not actually just sit at the water's edge and duck their faces, they will instead take a plunge into the water. They particularly like waterfalls but they have to be quite small waterfalls, otherwise the currents would be too strong for them. What they will eat are the leaves of what they have not used for their weaving practices.

Particular to the Trumpetears are their voices, they actually sing like birds, and they sing with long notes. Trumpetears can become quite dexterous in this response. They live for approximately the time that it takes for them to fully mature. They would never, ever not have an offspring during their life, so a Trumpetears will always have at least one offspring in it's lifetime. Although the males only bear offspring three times within their life cycle, the female will still always be able to find a male who will at least mate and produce one new Trumpetears for the two of them. In this way their numbers may well fluctuate. They may actually pass back to the spirit world at sometime between forty and eighty human years.

The whole idea behind what a Prima faerie is, is that it is the one representative of that particular group or tribe who happens to be more giving than anyone else. It may be that there are three or four others who are possible Prima faerie of that particular tribe of Trumpetears. It may well be that there will not be a single Prima at one time but there could be two, unlike other faerie group who actually only have one. The Prima Trumpetears will have a slightly different set of wings, which it will develop. What develops upon the wing is a small hook on the leading edge or forward edge of the wing pointing outwards. This hook will be like a small finger and is something that will be developed and point outwards or sideways, it will be approximately one inch from the beginning of the wing. The Prima faerie are always females and never males. They do not grow taller, they are only recognizable by this hook.

Their third eye colour turns to a rich emerald green that glows in the dark, in fact it glows all of the time. The other thing to note is that a Prima Trumpetears when it is in this situation does not necessarily always represent itself in a physical way. It is much of the time in a semi-etheric or spirit way, so that all that you see will be it's aura and the emerald green. It may be that through the ability of bonding with the infant or through the gift of giving in the upbringing or educating of the infant, the Trumpetears may gain the possibility of becoming a Prima Trumpetears.

The Trumpetears' dance is quite ingenious, it is as though they are playing hopscotch backwards when they dance and they will do this in pairs. So it is like they never actually meet when they are dancing because they are always working backwards and in different time to one another. Perhaps one of them will turn one way and the other one will always face opposite, but will never actually meet in their dance. We wonder if it is because their knees are facing backwards, that when they think they are going forwards, they are in fact going backwards – what do you think?

You cannot tell the difference between a male and a female other than the fact that the female has thumbs which although they are set in the middle of the wrist they are actually pointing forwards, whereas the male's thumbs are pointing backwards. The thumbs are still quite small, but they can still curl their hands into a proper ball, so they are still able to use the thumbs even though they are in the middle of the wrist.

They are associated with flowers from the Azaleas, Camellias and Rhododendron. They also are associated with other flowers that have trumpet like shaped flowers. Azaleas Camellias and Rhododendrons tend to grow in all kinds of forests and woodlands and are not restricted to the area in which they live. They may live either in the southern hemisphere, the northern hemisphere, within the equator, or in the tropics. They do have social gatherings at times which is usually tied into the lunar cycle. They are also affected quite closely by other planets, you will never ever see a Trumpetears out when Mars is present. We are told that they view Mars presence as an omen that is negative towards them. We are told that is the impression they have of that particular planet and only that particular planet. They are happiest when the moon is new.

They will very often wear a complete flower upon their heads and their ears will protrude out through holes in the hats. They take the rear spine of each leaf, that is if you break either an Azalea or a Camellia or even perhaps a Rhododendron leaf and peel off the main stem from the back of the leaf. This is something that is quite coarse, they will use their saliva to break down the very coarseness of the spine and this will cause it to be much more flexible. They will then use these as a form of weaving, they will twist them with their little fingers and pull them. It actually takes two to make this form of cloth. This form of material is a kind of a thread for the cloth they will weave, and what they will then do is they will set and make a structure from it. They will merely attach it to a stick and they will set the thread up as you would a wattle and daub! A fashion of weaving which is a form of ancient weaving. They will pass a shuttle backwards and forwards of a stick form and a simple cloth will be made. This cloth will become quite flexible and it will be fashioned into a fairly loose garment that they will attach to and around their shoulders.

Generally, they do not interact with other animals because they are shy and try to keep very much to themselves. When bees are present they get along well with them, but this is not to say of course that bees are the only beings that will pollinate flowers on our side of life, as butterflies, other flies, wasps, different kinds of bees will do exactly the same job as the honey bees. Although wasps are usually so grumpy that they are not so well liked by faerie groups of any kind, it is as though you have an insect that always has a bad hair day!

They do not get ill and so they do not succumb to illnesses in general. However, they are a little susceptible when and if levels of certain minerals are present or vibrations are specifically present that are uncomfortable for them. These are to do with lead and mercury since lead is a part of the process that contains a form of nuclear material. It is in fact the release of nuclear material that they dislike and would actually make them very ill. Insecticide when applied involves human error of making it impossible for the plant to continue its reproductive process in a normal way. Whether it affects the Trumpetears itself is another matter, if they feel that the environment in which they are living becomes too hostile, they will merely move away. The plant itself will then begin to suffer because it does not have the companionship of the Trumpetears. Plants are much happier when Trumpetears are with them, the same as it is with any form of plant on earth and their relationship with their faerie partner. Do not forget that it is always from a plant's point of view that it is very beneficial. They feel privileged if they are allowed to be of service to one of their faerie form who wishes to use their services temporarily.

They try to see that the correct soil is there so they would bring various other minerals that the plant needs. Do not forget that most of these plants live in quite an acidic or ericaceous soil, so it may be that a special combination of ingredients needs to be maintained. It tends to be that if the specific ground around the plant deteriorates to such an extent that the plant can no longer survive, it will be the Trumpetears' job to remove one of the plants or one of the flowers of the plant, or even perhaps a stem or a new shoot. They will break it off and take it somewhere else so that the plant continues to survive while the remaining parent plant will be allowed to pass. After all, the spirit of a plant may well be transferred by the processes of propagation from an actual shoot or even a seed.

Chapter 14 – Polimetri Faeries

"Ah see ababan", (this is Kreak – the common faerie language for) "We are here".

These of the world as yet untouched, by human hand,
More pure than prayer itself, throughout the land,
For faerie bring no energy or crime,
That may unseat the power of love, in thine hand.
We have the presence of those who seek to sweeten life,
Above all repose.

They are of Polimitri of which I speak,
Whose hands and lives are here.
Polimitri are faerie of two inches, no more.
They are of rounded heads, as you've never seen before.
And round eyes sharp and bright,
That glow florescent silver in the night.

Their cheeks are broad and shiny,
Like reflecting envelopes, that broaden the face.
They are always creased as if about to burst into laughter.
It is the only line that sits upon their face,
For no worries have they, in their race.
Polimitri have bodies too,
Which reflect the hue, of from where they come.

For some, are born in the podded plant.
And others, through the flower scent that Spring or May enhance,
Any genteel garden or where food does grow.
For they are faerie of the Pea, and the flower of Snow,
Or the flower of red as angry bean,
Or the flower of hope, of pinks and green.
Ah see ababan.

Sweet peas, if you remember are a wild flower and were the first born of the Polimitri faeries. Gradually these faeries developed and have adopted other initial plant species as a kind of surrogate mother, or as a happy relative. Polimitris are non-physical beings who have a physical time period. They are present usually for between five and seven seasons, by which time they have increased their desire to help one another to such an extent that, they cannot bear to be parted any longer in the physical world. So they move back into the spirit world where they can continue forever.

Sometimes their skin is a dusty lemon and at other times it may be pink, or flecked. If they are pink and flecked, the fleck would rise from beneath their arms and gradually become no more at the neck. Their neck would be fairly wide to support the round head, as I say their head is perfectly round. They have hair which tends to be green, and very often their hands will be green as well, not a sharp green, but bordering between green and yellow. They may have their nails yellow and rounded as well with green fingers. Their fingers are fairly long and have three joints. They are able to materialize and dematerialize when they wish. They have legs which have two joints at the knee and ankle, their ankles are actually able to flex the feet at ninety degrees in both directions, which gives them the ability to actually spin round on one leg without moving their foot.

Polimitri are most endearing, they have ears which are small, round and centrally located. The ears have a small lobe at the bottom which is faced inward. The ear only has one band which holds the ear outward, this is sat upon the very edge and in a sense is turned over toward the front. The ear is slightly smaller than you would expect, but being that Polimitris are very sensitive, they do not have to rely on very acute hearing or over sensitive hearing because they can pick things up through their fingers and toes.

They have wings which are four in number. The front portion is a pair of two which have fairly pointed tips, these wings are completely transparent but are covered with small green veins. The outside of their wings in the moonlight, would be seen as silver, just on the very far edge. They do give each other names but they have a terrible memory. So they keep reinventing who they are because they do not remember their own name, let alone someone else's! This of course, as you can imagine ends up being very confusing. They usually greet each other with "who are you, hello, who are you?"

They drink water captured from plant leaves. Sometimes they will sow a leaf together with a small strand of horse hair to capture the water within it, but more often than not they will simply suck the leaf or whatever moisture has been collected upon it by morning rain. They are assiduously clean and brush their teeth. They enjoy swimming and will bathe in small streams but they never go near stagnant water. The young Polimitri often eat small, young and fresh peas and will eat the pod as well. The pea and it's cycle may be some months long, and during this time the activity of Polimitris is quite noticeable. It may be that they are with a broad bean plant or a long bean plant as well as Sweet Pea and Sweet William.

Their tongues are actually quite pointed, although you would not see it very often and their tongues also tend to be, a feint dusty blue. Their eye irises are silver and round. What would have been the white of the eye ends up being a similar powdery blue like the tongue. The pupil is black, though the pupil itself does not open very far, it is actually quite small in relation to the rest of the eye. They do not have eyelids, which is why they shy away and cannot not blink. What they will tend to do is nap and go to sleep in the mid-day, but they do not close their eyes. Sometimes they sleep standing up so you do not know or realize if they are sleeping. They just have this long wistful vacant expression. What tends to happen is that their eyes fall downwards when they are sleeping, this is really the only way you can tell. The eyes actually move right down. Their eyes are quite large in any event, at least one and a half times bigger than a human's eye. They do have very thin eyelashes, which are just above the very top line of the eye. It is a row of fine hairs, with spaces in between them. They are not in clumps or clusters, they are just single hairs that are not too long. These are really to catch any dust particles that may drop towards their faces when they are flying.

The nose is small and pointed, which may seem strange when the face is so round. Generally, the nose has two small hovels at the bottom of it. The nose is not that long but there is quite a large gap between the bottom of the nose and where the mouth is. The mouth has thin lips which are red. The skin generally tends to be a powdery yellow or lemon, sometimes moving toward green in the lower half of the body, sometimes this arises from a pink or blushed stain that comes up from around the central chest area. This can have dark flecks upon it but is never black and the flecks can often be purple in colour.

They have a kind of hair which tends to be green, it is not long and usually not that thick either. At times the hair may have yellow tips upon it, these yellow tips gradually break off and that is why the hair is not that long because it actually governs itself. Their hair is perhaps a quarter of an inch long but remember they are only two inches tall! The wings at first are small sticky buds and do not actually come about until at least the end of the first week. This means until then they either ride upon a parent's back, or they can sometimes be found sitting on plant stems just waiting. The mothers do have small breasts, and they do give their offspring milk, but only in the first week. This is a faerie first, so far! They have bright auras, usually of a dusty pink, sometimes of blue, their aura moves to white and shimmers when they are really heavy.

Reproduction of the Polimitri is either through their flower or they adopt a particular peapod. The male and female Polimitri will eat the peas of a certain pod and then they will seal up most of the pod apart from one end. They will then leave a sticky secretion within the pod from their mouths and the female Polimitri will blow her life energy into it first, then followed by the breath and life energy of the male. It usually takes two to three nights for the Polimitri offspring to come alive. It is during this time that the parents are most protective, both of them will stay with the tenderling that they have brought about, which is what they call them. A tenderling will be no more than half an inch at first, but will then quickly sprout and grow. In just a few short weeks they will be exactly the same as a Polimitri in full flight.

They do not wear shoes or have any form of footwear at all. The clothes they wear are from dried leaves, which one would think would be rather stiff, but they are not because they cover them in a kind of oil which comes from tree bark. They mix it with a special saliva from their throats which makes it a more pliable nature so that they can spread it on to the leaf, and that will both preserve and keep it very pliable. Their clothes are made by Nictor Dwarfs who make many items of clothing which they take to faerie markets for resale! (Usually for sweet fruits or vegetables, that kind of thing). Nictor Dwarfs are also very small, and the one endearing feature about them is that they have long beards which are segregated into two pieces, with a gap in the middle where the chin would be. This is all we know about the Nictor Dwarfs at the moment. Polimitri clothes by the way are very tight upon them, they wear a kind of pant which is usually not all the way to their ankle because they like to keep their legs free of any inhibition. The bottom half of their legs are actually an admiring point for this particular faerie.

They never wear anything black, their clothing, which is made from leaves, is usually an off green, a pale green that has once been vibrant but obviously cannot keep it's pigment. They can sometimes be seen wearing a red petal which they put on a strand of horse hair and wear it about their necks. This usually comes from a flower of the pea family which has not yet turned into a fruit bearing pod. For their clothing, they will use the leaves of beans, these tend to be very good because they are so large and broad. They could actually make a whole item of clothing out of just one leaf as they are so small. They will gather them and then they will coat the leaves in this sticky substance mixed with their saliva, which generally tends to be the sap from trees, and they will then preserve it. They will leave them at a specific time and place for the Nictor Dwarf to come and retrieve them. The Nictor Dwarf does not have to measure them because it knows that all of the Polimitri are the same size as they do not vary.

They do dance and sing although their songs are not that tuneful. They have a song that sounds like a cricket and sometimes can be confused with crickets, as they do play with crickets. The young can very often be seen riding on the crickets' backs and they let out little 'wheeeeee' sounds as they play. Their language will depend on where they are, as Polimitris tend to follow language that is common to human beings of whatever country they are in, as they are all over the planet. There are hundreds of thousands of them, wherever there are these plants and vegetables, including the wild ones as well as the cultivated ones. In a way they are responsible for bringing sweet things to the harvest of human beings, but other beings depend on the fruits of this family and what they are trying to bring about for the good of other beings, not just for humans.

Chapter 15 – Water Faeries – The Salina Aqa Faeries

Salina Aqua is a different form of faerie, it is a faerie of the water world. Salina Aqa are beautiful, undeniably so. To look at Salina Aqa is to look at beauty in the truest sense.

To actually look at one brings great difficulty, they are almost transparent. How can something that transparent have a physical appearance? In some respects, Salina Aqa bring different definitions of what is cellular activity. They appear anywhere from just a few small inches in height to as much as eighteen inches in height. They have even been known to be larger than that, but none has ever exceeded twenty one inches. To describe them is a little like looking at a glass figurine. They have a human body shape that is noticeably thinner than most. They appear solely through coating themselves with water molecules, and are in true essence, spirit beings.

Salina Aqas do not breed as they merely exist. There are no new ones so they are all very ancient beings. They are not defined as being a race which breeds, rather it tends to be that those in the spirit world decide that Salina Aqa will be their journey. They are responsible for making water viable for other living organisms to exist within it's orders.

They may very often dress themselves in algae and wear it as a kind of jacket. They may even furnish themselves with clothing that appears green, or has a lucid green feel to it, which is somewhat milky in appearance. This is because at times they just wish to do that and display themselves in that colour which makes a change from being almost transparent. They have hands, fingers and jointed limbs which appear almost anywhere along the length of the arm or the leg. It is as though at any one moment the knee may be half way between the foot and at the bottom. They have toes that consist of three. Their hair appears to be regular in its arrangement. In other words a single strand is focused with lines of cells which reflect the colour. Salina Aqa appear to have the ability to simply melt into whatever background it presents itself in.

Salina Aqas are able to change their appearance as they wish. It does not change height, it merely uses these changes to be able to move itself into different corners or places. It is able to squeeze through the smallest gap, between pepples and, yet can stand before you, as I say many inches high. It is really through the memory, that the Salina Aqa wishes to portray, so that is what you see and observe. They will look as though they have three fingers as well as a thumb, which is almost a finger. The thumb faces backwards to the fingers and is used for grasping at reeds to hold onto in swiftly moving currents.

They do not eat things, yet they have a mouth with blue lips, a cross between turquoise and the blue of daylight sky. These lips are quite small but perfectly formed. The nose is gently pointed and shaped as though done with a fine sculpture's knife. If at all, their nose is a little more Romanesque than any other faerie that has been featured so far. They have quite large eyes which are round and perfectly blue. They have a quality about them, if you can see them for long enough. They hold you in a trance like state when you look upon them, or should we say when they allow you to see them. Their eyes can hold such a magic that would leave a human being transfixed. The iris is the part that is blue, you would not see the rest of the eye because it is transparent. They do have a pupil but it is only very slightly darker than the iris itself, looks infinite and always carries a white glow around it. They are the strangest eyes of all faeries because of the depth that this one particular blue seems to be able to magnify in

an unending journey. You could say it is a form of blue which is truly infinite. It is just the same as if you were looking into the daylight sky and seeing for the first time further into the vision of your future.

If a fish swims towards them, they merely allow it to swim right through them as they are able to change their cells dynamic shape. They change the way in which they are a part of one particular dimension or another and they merely move out of the way, but it appears as though a fish could actually swim through it. There is no particular gender of a Salina Aqa, although they appear to be female and is quite possibly due to situations to do with other forms of earth spirit. They do not always have the body of a female human but at times they can represent themselves as such. What they reflect is whatever they feel that day. They are most definitely telepathic, mainly using images. It appears that their use of images are quite liberal. They can transport images from one place to another over quite long distances, even hundreds of miles. Like many to do with water, they are able to transmit through the medium of water because it is very good at being able to carry even the faintest of sound, or the most vivid of pictures.

They have wings but they do not really need them, as they just enjoy the experience. They have forms of ears which have a small hole at the lower end which appears to be a way of hearing or magnifying sounds, for whatever purpose. The ears do not bend or move in any particular direction yet they are able to hear equally well behind them, as they can in front or even to the side. Their ears are small and round and they tend to be set at the centre of where their neck joins their head. They have a very definite head which actually has quite a humanoid shape to it. Their face is round, maybe more egg shaped than round. Their hair is quite regular and the hair is usually swept back. The hair goes from the head to the body, growing on the body into a type of V shape going down the back in a thin line of hair. These appear to be no more than an inch, maybe a little bit like a lion's mane. They do have a form of eyelid, though we cannot think of what use it would be? It seems that the eyelid closes from time to time, and then opens but again there is no particular reason for them. They do have a small row of ancillary hair on the eyelid which are very short and fine. Perhaps they are merely to keep dust particles from them when it is in turbulent water. Even when they are in this water they can still see through the eyelids, so they are there in fact as a precautionary measure and protective layer. They do not have eyebrows.

Sleep is not required and many do not even know what they do when they are not visible. They are very secretive and their lives are difficult to define. They are playful with each other and even with other creatures. They do not appear to age or degenerate in any way at all. There have been Salina Aqas upon the planet earth for thousands of years and they have been the same ones, so a true ancient form. They do not give each other names but they do greet one another by bowing. They have a dance that they bring, and they do so by facing one another placing their heads upon one another's shoulders alternately, very similar to the way swans do. They do not display any other forms of physical contact.

They tend to have an aura which varies between different shades of pink. This is very similar to their skin colour, but it seems that their skin colour actually radiates out several inches around their figure form. It appears that the radiation is a form of very delicate pink to white. They do not have a Prima Salina Aqa and those in the spirit world decide who will become a Salina Aqa. There is not a particular species or breed of spirit who are affiliated with or attached to Salina Aqa. It is merely an attraction of choice to some spirit who wish to have that experience.

The only time when humans in the physical world may ever see them is when they are transitioning from one state to another. They are associated with fresh water only and are very fond of waterfalls, rapids and any swiftly moving water which brings large amounts of oxygen to the surface. That doesn't mean to say that they need oxygen in order to survive, for they do not actually need to breath or have anything to do with a physical state at all. They merely exist as the memory that they wish to portray.

How is it that it gains energy to propel itself, or gain energy for anything? Well, to be quite honest there is an exchange of hydrogen, of other different chemicals that appear to allow it greater movement. Oxygen rich states are also something that appear to give it benefit in it's movement, so that is perhaps why they are more frequently seen around waterfalls, faster flowing rivers or water activity, simply because these are places where oxygen rich environments thrive. Salina Aqas do not need water in order to transfer themselves from one place to another, they merely vanish and reappear elsewhere, or wherever the mood takes them. It may not be on this planet, it would be wherever there is water, but always where there is fresh water. When confronted with polluted waters, they very sadly tend to move on. They will even sometimes blend with large downpours of rain and use that as a way of moving away from heavily polluted areas. They only return when harmony is restored in the polluted areas. Waterfalls and streams in gardens may attract them, especially the smaller variety.

If you are able to look at them for long enough, you will observe that there is a very fine web of loosely woven thread that appears to be all over them when they are excited. And this web is the most sparkling violet which shines and twinkles in the light of it's own state, like a loose veil. It is not finely or closely woven you understand, there can be quite large spaces around it, although it seems to be almost like it has brought a spider's web around itself at a time when it is happy. Salina Aqa cannot have power over water but joins with it in order to bring about a resolution of purity. It is difficult to define how many Salina Aqa would actually occupy a particular stretch of river. They may actually help water escape the confines of earth, perhaps creating a new spring pushing through the soils to actually bring about new channels. It has been known that a Salina Aqa takes on the shape of a fish, or has from time to time shaped itself like a water plant merely so that it can keep within the same vibrations of physical form. This allows them to observe in a physical way the actions that some other beings are creating on physical earth.

Chapter 16 – Water Faeries – The Salina Aqa Minorette

Minorette are to do with the Salina Aqua family, but is actually quite different in the source of spirit, of who that Minorette is, of who that spirit really is in the scheme of things. Minorette suggests small, and they are small, but perfectly formed. They grow only to between one and three inches in total height. They have a human feel to them, it may well be that they are heavily associated with those beings who at one time were a part of the formation of the union between human beings. They are not still birth, so they are not to do with any of those who have reached fuller maturity within the relationship of spirit and humanity, such as those in the later stages of the gestation period. They are mainly to do with those fetuses who never get past a few months of physical life for whatever reason that maybe. The spirit of this experience does not try to have another experience, but after several generations of humanity have past; they are invited to become Minorettes, so that is what they are. Past generations that so often drew them or painted them, gave a false impression of what a Minorette is really like.

They do not have baby type form or small infant form but they have small children form and never go beyond that. They never become an adult Minorette, they remain as a small child form. They will have all of the qualities that a physical representation of a child would have, and they are a slight dusty pink in colour. They have round eyes which actually have points at the corners with horizontal lines upon their faces. Their eyes are large compared to their faces, the eye is at least half as large again as a human eye. Their irises tend to be a cross between salmon pink moving toward violet and their pupils are black with a white star in the middle. The eye colouring and shape will be the same in all Minorettes. They do not have eyebrows that grow but have eyelashes and eyelids very similar to humans. It is the shape and style of their eyes that make them so unique.

Sometimes they have an aura which is powder blue and can be seen from quite some distance. In fact that will be the first thing a human being would see, if they had a chance to see one! When in fact their colouring appears to be a dusty pink, they are actually semi translucent. At times when they are happiest, their aura turns to a bright light, quite a bright white light really, and that is because they are so full of joy. They are in a way etheric because they are spirit, however they are physical in body. They do not die and pass, they merely get bored with where they are, or the water in their area has been drained and they migrate elsewhere. They do need water to be shown or seen in a physical state. They can disappear at will and turn up somewhere else.

They do drink occasionally, drinking from the water just because it allows lubrication of their voices, and they do have voices. They do not talk in pure Kreak, they speak very much in the words or the language in which they were associated in spirit. This is related to their temporary embodiment of the human side of life, as they do carry the genetics from humans. If they are living in a particular place, does it mean to say then that they may have migrated? Well yes, absolutely so, they may have migrated from somewhere else upon earth.

They do have wings, but sometimes they fold them up, or the wings fold up themselves. They do this by rolling them up within themselves, up towards the shoulder blades. When they wish to fly they poke them out like tongues. Their wings are fairly short and are pointed at the end. They have two sets of wings which point at a forty five degrees angle from the perpendicular of the body. These wings begin slightly lower on the back than many others, just below the shoulder blades and the wings both extend at the same angle. So you have two sets of finger like wings, they are not large, they are flat but they are finger like and transparent

in their appearance and similar in style to Dragonfly wings. They have small veins running through them which are between a salmon pink and red to the tip. So you can see with their powder blue aura they are quite impressive and beautiful to look at.

They have hair of human appearance and so similar to the way in which they would have been coloured had they continued to have had a human experience. They will still follow that genetic line exactly the same as though they had continued to maturity as a child. Their hair does not really grow and some of them may have much less hair on their head and look much smaller in their appearance.

They have ears that are not pointed or any strange shape as they will be exactly as they would appear for a human being. There is one difference, however, and that is the lobe of the ear will be elongated by almost as half as much as the ear itself. Their skin will be pink or yellow or black or however the genetics of the child manifestation would have become. So all of those genetic features that would have appeared within the human species would be transposed into the Minorette. Their noses are as you would expect to see, as would be the mouth. Their mouths more often than not would be of a very delicate texture, they will have small teeth, and they will have tongues the same as they would have had. Minorettes' main difference to human beings are that they have wings. Their fingers are completely intact and they are very fond of drawing on one another's lips. They will use certain plants in order to produce different natural coloured dyes. They will even go so far as to use different sorts of mud in order to grind minerals together to bring different colours out to the surface. They can make oak or different colours from sandstone or sediments that may be around in where they live.

A typical scene of them is that they would be sitting on a bank swishing their feet on the water backwards and forwards, talking and laughing amongst themselves. They love to swim, they love to be within the water as well, and they have no problem with either environment as they do not actually have to take a breath for air. Although they will have that mechanism if they want to talk or sing. They sing because they like to and they sound like children singing. Their word of greeting is 'Twoalla' and 'Shotoo' is their word for goodbye.

During a regular day they will go about their business which tends to be that they wash if they wish, or as children they may not. They like to play and they spend a great deal of time playing together. They have games of tag and chase and are very quick both in water and in the air. They use their arms and legs for swimming to propel them through water, or they may use their minds to bring them suddenly to somewhere else. What good do they actually bring? Well, they bring their ambient energy. They do not physically mend or fix things, their presence is not to do with that. Their presence is to do with the well-being and stability of the place itself so their presence is to do with their quality.

They live in clear fresh water marshes and bog regions all over the planet. They can tolerate brackish water as well. Brackish water is when salinity has risen and there is a certain quantity of salt, or it may also be mixed with various large quantities of clear fresh water. So they may inhabit many different regions on earth but they particularly enjoy those regions of peat and that kind of high level of the aquifer. As it is they live in areas where there is high drainage so that the aquifers are actually showing themselves on the top of the surface rather than being under underlying rock formations. They do not live within these underlying aquifers as that belongs to another type and species of faeries.

These beings can put aside their egos, their will of right of all beings in this matter because Minorettes enjoy the company of each other. There could be perhaps two to three hundred living in one particular region that may perhaps be a peat bog. There are many of them that live in Ireland, particularly southern Ireland. Sometimes people try to hunt for them, as it would be a prize indeed to capture one. However they are very wise, having actually been engaged with the possibility of human life they understand very much about human life and the integrities that people have, along with the behaviors that people also tend to have. They are most enlightened by it and so they are very wary of human beings and what their motivation is in being near them. As you can imagine their world is very quiet because bogs being the type of places which are really just silent with perhaps only birds, flowers, different mosses and other forms of life that may not inhabit other places.

They will wear forms of clothes that are made for them by other beings. The clothes tend to look like practical garments. Once they actually put the physical garments on, they then exhibit the same habits as that of the wearer. The clothes are actually spun, woven material and may be wool from sheep. It may be that they actually use other materials that are perhaps cast off by humans and are merely re-fashioned into clothing for them. Although these garments begin life as physical clothing that humans may have worn or from other creatures, they have grown physically so that they have an element of genetics. They have an element of cellular division within them because they are physical things, with the same physical properties they would have had. Once Minorettes put the clothing on, the clothing will instantly take on the same characteristics as the Minorette has and be able to vanish along with the Minorette. Otherwise you would have just small suits of clothes walking around with nothing in them. Although sometimes they do that as well just for fun, the Minorettes will at times be able to switch off this link between their clothing and themselves. However, they very rarely wear shoes.

Very often Minorettes may be seen riding on frogs, and that is a great source of joy. They have great empathy with amphibians because they themselves do not have a mind to harm anything, even though the frogs may accidentally eat one another occasionally. So you can see then that Minorettes are like children, they have minds like children, but they also have a wisdom and awareness well beyond their generation. Animals can see them so they play with whatever is with them. Their lives are of joy as they are not of any other form of emotion or vice because their lives are pure, and that is something always to remember. Their lives remain pure, as pure as a Minorette can be.

They do not become ill or do not die. They could be here on earth as long as they wish, just returning to the spirit world when they feel that way. They tend to live in both worlds, it will depend on what they want to do at the time. Eventually their thoughts may change and they may give up this aspect of their life as this happens, and move on to something else as the spirit being they are.

Minorettes are such pure beings, since they have not been tainted by the human experience as it were in the flesh. It means that their presence can bring abundant loving energy toward things. This is really something that they find great use for, so they will be present at times of healing. Minorettes are one of the great healers of the spirit world, which is a little known fact! They will be present during many situations of emotional healing that happen in the spirit world, to do with those that may have to make transitions from their physical state to their continued spirit life, perhaps a past with some dreadful disease or something like that.

What happens is that a great concentration of help is required to bear upon that spirit individual to resolve issues of mind and consciousness, entrapped by one's experience of physical life and of how one passed into spirit. Minorettes are very often present during these times giving their energy and help. This is something that they graduate to, it is a decision that they make, so they are very much implicated in the lives of all of us in the spirit side of life.

Before the spirit becomes a fully entwined Minorette, it will follow through the whole human experience in the spirit world. It will continue it's relationship with those parents or the Mother who was primarily responsible for forming the physical being. This relationship will continue and will still be a part of the Minorette's life, it is not something that is lost. The Minorette is in fact a different embodiment, if you like of the child that would have existed, but continues to exist in the spirit world. At the same time, Minorettes can also decide that they wish to continue upon their pathway and not have a return visitation in the form of a Minorette with physical experiences on earth. Minorettes are very often responsible for the engagements between spirit, children and human beings, as well as having their function in the bog like places.

Minorettes because of their healing and giving abilities will help those spirit children to manifest themselves for their parents or aid in their communication with human beings, although they do not actually present themselves, as they will keep themselves in the spirit world. Spirit children may be drawn back to engage with the physical world for the sharing of love or the sharing of their relationships, particularly for those parents who are so bereaved by their loss. They may well take on the names that their Mothers had in mind at the time. This will be an issue of love that has grown between the Mother and child, even though the child was never physically realized, as that relationship does continue. It is important for people on our side of life to understand this.

Chapter 17 – Water Faeries – The Salina Aqa Majoriae

The Salina Aqa Majoriae are similar in voice and form, though their parentage is not. The Majoriaes are in fact quite exquisite and I will try to describe their physical appearance as I see them. They are between four and eighteen inches in height, though we understand some have been known to be taller, as tall as twenty inches. They wear a form of clothing which appears to be like silken thread, yet it is not like a material seen before. The material is light, it seems to flow quite sensibly in the direction that they are swimming or have swum from, and it is their swimming that we have to pay particular attention. The Majoriaes have four fingers and a thumb which are webbed, a little like a frog, I suppose. Their thumb is an extended finger, it isn't shorter, but longer than all of the others.

Their feet are webbed the same as their hands, and they have five toes. The central toe which is the third from the inside of the foot, is the longest. Their height is including their toes, so if you stretched one out completely flat with the arms by the side that would denote the height. When they are swimming their toes point backwards. They also have small fin like apertures at their knees, these appear to be raid fins very similar to fishes. It is quite extraordinary because they are completely etheric, yet they can maintain their physical state for a considerable time. It does not appear to be a conscious effort for them to do that.

Their hair has a fine thread like appearance and seems to appear in different shades of blonde to black and even white. White hair does not seem to denote age, but what does denote age is the white crescent at the crown of their heads. The crown is the centre of the oval shaped head which has its longest point at the lower front of the face. They appear to have lips that are pink. The skin of those I see is a mixture, and we are told it will depend entirely upon where they are living at the time. As they migrate they change their skin tone to match the environment wherever it is they are travelling to. It is to say that although they are etheric beings they do not use their hybrid status, as it were, to travel because they enjoy swimming so much. They like having a physical experience, it is something that brings them great joy and responsibility.

The Majoriaes have large eyes, at least twice the size of a human being in relation to their face. Their skin colour then tends to change and alter depending on where they are at the time. It can move from white to green to blacks or even reds depending upon the background of the environments, as they do not wish to stand out too much. One would think that the Majoriaes would prefer the tropical waters of the warmer climates, but this does not appear to be so, they seem to be happy in either cold or warm waters. I am well aware that you would not have coral in cold water, but what you would have in colder water are the many various fishes and the many different properties of the kelp forests, where many of them like to spend much of their time.

They have the appearance of having hair which seems abundant. They say they rarely have it cut, and if they do, it is through the presence of a particular fish, the Pilot fish, who inhabit and share their existence with whales and sharks. In some places Pilot fish are known as 'cleaner' fishes in the sea world, their work is actually shared with Parrot fish, who live in more brackish water. These fish help to maintain the Majoriaes' appearance. Their hair appears to be long, thin strands, much like human hair and it tends to move with the water as you would expect it to. They often may be found in silent and still poses, as though contemplating their next situation, their next thought, or waiting for an idea to come to them and then suddenly they will disappear. It isn't that they have necessarily disappeared, but they

are able to swim with a flick of their legs a great distance.

Their eyes are set in the middle of their heads, at the front pointing outwards, directly outwards. They have a cleft above the eyes and a forehead which is somewhat extended. The hairline is in an arc, indeed the hair does not actually start until the centre of the head, where the glowing iris of their star begins to form. This is a white glowing orb that gradually, over a period of time, becomes brighter and more accentuated. This seems to be the only sign of them aging. It appears that they gather information and harvest it as someone else would harvest food. They bring this as a record of their lives, as well as, a record of the planet itself, of that medium of the planet. The star is right at the crown of the apex of the head, where the hair begins in a rounded journey from ear to ear. It is a bright white star, gradually shining more and more. It does have a form of a flap which extends from the front of the star over it, when it wishes to be inconspicuous. Normally when they are swimming or doing anything, the star will be quite visible. The star is quite bright and helps them see better in the dark, but they do not have a star when they first appear in the physical state. It seems to develop after the second or third year of their existence but even then it is only as a small bud. It does not actually glow at all and it takes at least ten to fifteen years for the star to have any effect upon the surroundings.

Their eyes are very often seen as an iridescent greenish blue, which tends to have flecks of deep blue within it around the iris. It has a dark pupil centre, it does not have white around the outside and it is transparent where the iris would be. The eye is quite round and they always look as if they are staring right at you. They do have a form of eyelid and it blinks from the top and the bottom and meets in the middle. They do not have eyelashes but what they do have is a very thin membrane which appears as a flap from the upper eyelid at the time when they are asleep. Therefore, this closes the eye completely and seals it, a kind of an inner eyelid. It is as though this does not extend at any time unless they are actually sleeping. When they are sleeping, this other membrane unravels itself over the bottom eyelid, as though it is drawing a blind upon itself. To look at them when they are sleeping, it seems as though they only have one eyelid extending from the top all the way to the bottom. It is really quite different to any other creature or being in this respect. If you were to look at the cleft above the eyes from the side, it appears that the forehead is accentuated by the cleft, the forehead then sweeps back to the crown where the hair starts.

They have joints in their arms and their legs and have an ankle and a knee that appear to have a bottom at the top of their legs. Their ears are extremely small as they are just very small flaps of skin. As they swim they flap them backwards and forwards as they are going against the back of the head. The ears do point backwards, although they can hear perfectly well all the way round. They tend to use sonic vibrations in order to pick up sounds and as a form of location device as well. The ears are round, although they have filaments of skin which appear to be undulating in their appearance. It is as though these flaps of skin which extend from the ears backward do not have a particular outline. They are quite ragged as though someone has bitten pieces out of it. Although it does not seem to be that it is wearing out, they all seem to have this but just different for each one. You can see the orifice in the ear but it is quite small and unprotected. There does seem to be a small protrusion at the front of the ear, like a small bud. This bud is round and is at the same position upon the head as the hole itself. So if you were looking at the ear you would have the bud first, then the hole, and then the ear encased around it. The ear is completely round, although it is as though it is off centre. So you have the small bud to begin with and then next to that you have the hole of the ear, from the nearest point between the bud and the hole of the ear is where the ear flange actually begins.

Their nose is small, cute and round at the end. It looks to be forming from the ridge described above the eyes and it merely just extends down very similar to a Romanesque nose. Although there is a dip in between where the nose starts and the actual ridge across the top of the eyes. They have small nostrils which close, each nostril has a flap of skin which has an opening in a vertical position which is called a clef by the faeries themselves. Their clef opens and closes as they so wish, when sensing something or identifying an essence in the water. They are also able to hear with their noses at times, as this is because when their clefs are open they are able to bring the sound in to their minds and consciousness.

Their mouths are quite wide and have a row of teeth at the top which are quite square. They appear to have two rows of teeth, at the front of the bottom which are very close together. We are told this is so they can just scrape the surface of kelp or some other organic plant without damaging the internal structure of the plant. They are very delicate eaters and the bottom teeth do extend back along the jaw line. Their lips are thin and pink while the mouth goes to a point at the top of each corner. They do not have an indent at the top of their lips like human beings, they just follow the curve around much like a human bottom lip would. They smile quite a lot but the whole mouth does not open wide to full width unless they are laughing. They have a form of tongue which is round at the tip, extends only a short way from the mouth, and is used to help move food around the mouth whilst they are eating.

They appear to sing and in tone thoughts of their ancestry, very similar to whales and in this way you could say they do seem to have a form of language. It is not Kreak, though they communicate with many other species. As we understand it, they communicate pictorially, through something called alpha sound which enables them to send a thought from their minds. And, yes we know that thought is language, but it can also be that they send a picture of something they wish to create, or of a relationship they wish to construct showing the emblems of different creatures or beings that they want to communicate with. They then send this alpha sound image to the other beings or creatures they wish to communicate with. They do not have wings but they have fins instead on the outer edge of their knees. They also have a fin on each side of their hip, or where a hip would be although this is a very small fin but it is quite strong and aids in their swimming ability.

The Majoriae faeries tend to be mainly females, which is a curious thing. We are told males do exist but they are forever in the etheric or spirit world and they do not actually have a physical existence. They tend to stay in the region for eighty to a hundred years, which is quite a long time. They do not breed as such, but in physical state new ones appear from the ether world. The females have a physical appearance whereas males do not, but they may have a presence. The other aspect about their presence for the males is that they act as a form of door keeper or guardian angel, if you like. They tend to alert them to any possible danger. They are monogamous and in that respect life long, which is to infinity. They do not appear to have an aura, all the energy seems to be concentrated in the star on their head, which is actually called a 'sshatha'. The fins on their hips are clear, all fins are clear along with their webbed fingers and toes.

They do have individual names, but not as humans have. In the ether world these particular beings already have an auric identity, this is something that is transferred and added to if they have some small peculiarity of difference between one another. They will use these differences to enhance their name. So it might have an appendage of say 'round ears' or 'brown light' to denote a colour or inflection of some part of their anatomy.

They do have an upper and lower body but have a body form which does not have breasts, yet it appears quite human like in appearance. There is a neck which is quite short in some, whilst in others is longer. One would think small members of this group would be so exquisite and yet even the larger members of this group are just as so. They do appear to grow larger merely by the number of years they have been in existence. They all come here small and through their eating they do seem to grow.

They exist from the seashore to four hundred feet out in the ocean, this is approximately the limit of their habitat. They are really on the edges of the ocean as they do not venture into the deeps. As far as any continental shelf happens to be, they live around coral and play a particular part in the care. So you could say they are quite significant, particularly in our present day and age, because of the ways in which depletion and the change in atmospheric conditions have allowed greater bleaching from the sun to impact upon these life forms. It is not to say that the Majoriaes are troubled by this themselves because they are etheric. The Majoriaes are in fact wholly etheric, yet they have physical representations of themselves from time to time. They can use these physical representations to help those beings who live in and around coral reefs, the shallows surrounding islands, kelp beds and those kinds of aquatic places. They are often in company with sea lions and can sometimes be seen swimming with them and may even hold onto them at times for a ride.

One of the things they like to eat is in fact, kelp! They graze upon it, but they only seem to eat very small amounts. They are very careful which pieces they break off, they never take a whole kelp leaf, or a whole of anything else. They just have a little piece here and a little piece there. They do not want to harm or damage the plant they are feasting upon and they always ask permission before they begin. They always look for the youngest shoots and are very careful not to eat the tip so the plant can continue to grow, they really just nibble at the sides. Why then do they need to eat at all if they are etheric? It is quite simply that in order to show their physical state they need to bring something of the physical state into themselves, otherwise they would always remain etheric. If they actually eat something that is physical they do not have to expend so much energy in having a physical appearance. They can still vanish at will as it does not inhibit that aspect of their life, it just merely means that they are able to cope with different situations in a more realistic way. They can actually physically move objects, and so this means they can help more in the service of others.

Their clothing flows beyond the body itself and tends to gather at the back. It is most odd that they are able to wear such a thing which never actually seems to grow old or tired. It appears as a covering at any time but you do not see them without it. They do not have to wash as they live in water. They sometimes decorate themselves using abandoned shells. They do quite like shells because it contains substances which make it harder than anything they have themselves. It is actually creative for them making necklaces or bracelets. It tends to be small pieces of shell rather than a whole which would be cumbersome to them. We are told their appearance is quite magical!!

What do the Majoriae do? Well, they have many tasks trying to keep the equilibrium of where they live, so that all other beings are able to share it. They are most concerned with the destruction of the ocean, flora and fauna. They are well aware that there are natural situations which occur, which mean changes in the environment. They are also very mindful of the pressures of various kinds of pollution which actually disturb the innate qualities of the ocean floor, particularly those of the shallower reaches where many fishes live.

As you may be well aware, creatures of the sea tend to live to the extent of their ability that others allow them. It is a very hostile environment as many human beings see it. They decipher and gain opinions of the sea because they may not actually know of the real effort behind all of those organisms that live there, not just to feed on one another but actually to try to keep the whole organism in a healthy balance so their young may continue to survive in that region. They bring their efforts to bear on the smallest thing such as to try to find another shell for a whelk or a hermit crab who has been de-housed by another. Sometimes they may even be seen to sift through sand and pick out small particles of food left by other creatures. They would never, ever think of attacking another creature, they would never dream of doing such a thing, for they are there to preserve the integrity of all things. They may sometimes eat the odd morsel of what has been left by the many different actions that become unraveled in the sea life.

They do not mix with other faerie, they are quite content with their own company and type. It is not that they do not wish to communicate with them, as they would if urgent matters arose. What they will do is call a meeting which it is called a 'Claff' in which to share experiences. As you can well imagine, it would be something of a spectacle to see many thousands of Majoriaes together. Depending on where they have come from they may all be different colours. They will actually come together to provide information on various areas of where they live and to talk about how different beings are evolving in their lives, as they have great interest in the evolutionary process. They share this information so they may be more fore-armed as to how situations may blossom on their horizon. It is actually quite difficult at this present time because the weather patterns are so interchangeable, so very difficult to predict, that their meetings have been postponed on a number of occasions because of the change in the climate. This in itself does not bode well for the immediate future of the earth's environment and inhabitants. They are fully intent on understanding and unraveling the full relationship between themselves and all beings of the ocean.

Chapter 18 – Water Faeries – The Salina Aqa Allumniae

Listening to Gregory dictate these words is really quite moving. He says with tears flowing down the cheeks of his human counter-part or medium, "I feel like a lesser being in the presence of those who are here, not because they make me feel so, but that in spite of all I do, all I try to create, I am but who I am, whilst others dwell in the light of their own existence, such as these faerie we are to talk of today. These are the Salina Aqa Allumniae faeries. Just seeing them brings tears to my eyes, when visible it is as though you are looking at one of those greatest magical experiences you could ever hope to dwell within. My praise of them is not merely that I understand their motives but their very compassion. For the observance of all things that allow creatures made manifest in physical form who are able to bring sometimes devastation to one another, yet they are compassionate for all".

The Salina Aqa Allumniaes are these illuminous spirit beings who have a temporary physical appearance, they have in viewing them, a form of aura which is difficult to define. Their physical states may mimic almost any animal within the sea, so it may be that these illusive beings appear as a seal, a sea lion or a walrus. Their normal domain would be the deep sea. It may be that you aspire to catch one but it is an impossibility. Very few things are impossible, but with these it really is the case. This is quite simply because Allumniae are transparent when they wish to be, they may have the merest tint of blue or pink and they can arrange their cellular structure to almost any form. Their base structure happens to be that they have arms and legs, yet much of the time it may appear as though they themselves are intransient at the time of viewing them. It is as though they cannot quite make up their mind what they want to be or whom they wish to depict. So it is strange that you could be looking at a face almost of a human like form, and then it uses a morphic description to transfer itself into a sea lion.

Now when I say that their skin may appear to have a tint, it can be that Salina Aqa Allumniaes are in a state of at oneness or peace, in which case it will shine an iridescent blue. This blue does not glow within, but merely stays upon the surface. So it is as though you are looking through a being of liquid glass that has a reflected image which you can only vaguely see because of the blue of the surrounding and the vibrancy of their skin. Interestingly, sometimes when they appear in their human form, what actually gives them away are the small blue lights around their heads. These small blue lights are in fact the ends of their hair and what occurs is that the light from within them shines through the hair filaments and creates an orb at the end of where the hair ceases to be. You can imagine that when they are in the water, their normal domain would be the deep sea, and when they live in this place it actually has an effect as though you were seeing a cluster of stars.

Their eyes do tend to give them away and the reason they do so is because the iris is of a deepest, deepest purple blue. There is a ring around the outer edge of the iris which is fluorescent green. This ring is made up of small droplets of cell structure which gives the iridescent feel to it. They are like crystals and the central part of the eye is completely black. There is no other colour within the eye at all. It tends to be more rounder than a human eye and much larger, almost as though you were looking at a seal. If they metamorphosed into a seal, their eyes would indeed give them away. Their eye is the only element that does not change it's state. This and their auric field is how you determine what they are and the presence of what you are looking at. Their eyelids mimic humans exactly in that respect as do some other functions.

Their nose could be a human representation, with a mouth that would be quite small. At times they are able to elongate their mouth so that it extends from the face in the form of a trumpet with lips upon the end similar to that of a seahorse. The lips may extend half as long as the face. They do this to browse into the sandy bottoms of the ocean floor to make sure the nutrients that are within are all that they could be. It is something that happens when they are trying to find ecological reasons as to why certain events maybe occurring within the ocean. So you can imagine they are particularly busy at this present time.

They do not ever have wings, so people may say they are not really a true faerie, but they are, because they are in fact the pre-emptive faerie of all beings in a way. They do have a connection with all things, so they understand many of the nuances of how different beings have become interactive with one another within their life cycle. Salina Aqa Allumniaes are an almost perfect being. I say almost as no detriment to themselves, I am saying it as plainly as I might. What actually happens in their behaviour depends entirely upon what they wish to achieve that day, or that hour, or that moment. They do not actually regard day or night, because where they live is in perpetual darkness, yet where they exist is in a place covered in light. They are very cold beings to the touch, or to be around you.

They may vary in size from eight inches to as much as six or seven feet. The actual shape of a Salina Aqa Allumniaes are varied, but to be honest it has at times arms, legs, fingers and toes. (For the moment we will go with that description!) In their truest form they do not necessarily present themselves as having a human face. It may be that they have a representation of a human body, yet have a walrus face, or a sea lion face or in fact they may even have the face of some other being as yet unknown to medical science, to the botanists or to anyone who may be observing life forms of the faunic world on our side of life.

They may be in this guise for a very long time, as this form of Salina Aqa Allumniaes are known to be in existence for hundreds of years. It may be that they never fully disappear at all, as it is not as though they have a known quantity or that there are only so many. It appears that spirit who have become greatly illuminated within the path of all things in creation, simply at one stage or another develop their gift of transient behaviour. This is something that is brought about through the very real dynamics of giving to another being. Much like those of the soul group, much like those beings who orchestrate many other matters in other dimensions of space or time.

Telling a male from female tends to be that in all females there will be a small but very definite illumination at the base of the throat. This illumination will be the colour of frost pink. It is as though you were to take a clear crystal and put a dusting of white over a faint pink background. This dusting of white sparkles itself as small flakes, as though she is wearing a bead on her throat. This is not something that appears as a form, if you looked at it from the side view, it is in fact a mere bump upon the surface.

They do not wear clothes. They do depict themselves as male and female when they are in any shape or form, although they do not have a specific gender. They are merely representing what they are illuminating at that time. They are illuminated by their almost pale opacity, it is as though you are looking at a liquid glass figurine or something made of crystal which you would find almost flawless. The very fact that you can sometimes see them is because they have moved and the reflection changes.

They do not have a language as such, or do not appear to, although they are able to communicate in all things. When they speak to each other they may speak in their own tones of sharing mental images. They are telepathic breeders, that is they breed their own images of understanding as though they were playing a whole film. They are able to portray not just a particular image but a whole enactment as though they are staging a play for others to see.

They do at times have social gatherings, particularly when there are pressures mounting upon the environment. They are bound by their duty of care to keep it in as pristine condition as they are able. Naturally of course, if there are other environmental pressures which may bring harm to the whole realm then this is something that brings great consternation. They have the ability to look into the probabilities of what the future may bring. For the moment, it just happens to be that it is through their warnings, for their understandings of future events, which help to alert and send signals around our planet. This actually saves many physical lives, it alerts many fishes to descend to deeper depths, or to move away from a specific place.

They do not represent any plant form or specific animal group. They do not suffer from the pressures of the deep because they do not really have all of their being within it. They are merely a physical representation of how they wish to explain themselves at that moment, purely because they wish to observe many situations from different animals' viewpoints. By doing this they actually take on the animals' mannerism in order to try to discover and explain those very differences in their behaviors to others. It is basically that their presence creates the harmonics that is possible to be achieved within the oceans of our world. It means that because of them, there is not one single being that will ravage everything and that behaviors are kept only to the needs of sustaining their own lives. They do not tryst with want and behaviour. Many animals who become arrogant in their way simply because they have ceased to exist with their spirit, are merely reminded or perhaps marshalled by these Salina Aqa Allumniaes to be more considerate and caring as beings. It is as though they are the 'Care Bears' of the ocean world, bringing great illumination to all things they do.

Now at times they may move their shape and form into something that is quite distinctively odd, as though this present description is not odd enough! Sometimes they use their form to depict a different life form entirely, in which case they are not displaying their look in any way the same as a known animal might appear. They can in fact appear as though they are an anemone and have many tendrils upon their heads. They clasp onto a stone when they are doing this, which incidentally is very rare, but it is only really when they are wishing to blend with a specific life form that they feel is in trouble in some way due to the environment. They will transmit themselves into this completely different life form to try to gauge and understand what is physiologically and biologically going wrong with this particular form. Such as, why is it not functioning as well as it might? It is then able to organize the ability of that organism to perhaps migrate to another place where they might live. They cannot leave their place of birth, but their spores are gathered up and taken to a different place. They might try to change the environment or bring other beings in to enact upon it so as to alter it back again to a safer harmonic environment for that creature to inhabit.

They take on the whole persona of that being, and that includes their methods of communication to others who may join, in order to understand behavioral problems or situations that come about. So for example, they may decide that they wish to be a young whale so as to join a pod and understand what is happening with that particular being. As you can well imagine, a great mission of wisdom would occur, because whales almost definitely have such a strength, an inner understanding of universal breadth. It may well be that they adopt the form of such a creature for quite a while, because some whales are actually very slow to react to any particular thing, depending of course on the breed. Some are more vibrant than others,some are readier than others to bring their intellect to the surface and show it. Seals and Sea lions on the other hand are very vibrant and exuberant with their behaviour and the Salina Aqa Allumniaes will naturally adopt all of these characteristics because they are echoing that shadowed form so that they may learn more about that particular pod. The other animals may or may not recognize the faeries in their new form. Some seals and whales are very conscious and honoured by their presence. They may also do this to preside over some particular difference between some species and try to resolve these differences.

They do not have specific relationships favoring one above all others. They show great affection for one another at all times, though this is not transmitted as a physical act. They will sometimes appear as more than one, perhaps three or four, or even five and will re-enact a certain situation that may occur in ocean life. Not the eating of another animal obviously, but a certain form of habitat so that they may better acquaint and orchestrate themselves because their pattern is always that of learning. At times they will work in groups.

In shallower oceans you may only have very rare visitations of the faeries. This is simply because they prefer deeper water which is their home environment. To many of course, this environment may appear as though it is endless, like an endless barren desert, but it is not at all. There will be many crevices, many undulations, strata, rocks and different other beings who live there. Just the same as we have valleys and communities in certain places so it is in the sea and the oceans that life is depicted in the same way. These beings have always been spirit, it is as though they are a different form of a 'Shining one'. If they were not having a physical experience here on earth they would be visiting other worlds in their spirit form. They are not just on earth as it is something that is intrinsically bound.

The Sasquatch Mother and Child

One evening I was taken to meet and view a very special couple, where it was I do not know. I am told it was quite a privilege and it certainly felt like it.

We arrived in a small valley, similar to the small valleys made by eskers on the barren lands north of the tree line in northern Canada. The eskers were maybe thirty feet in height with scattered five to ten feet glacial size boulders dotted about. I cannot pin it down exactly where it was we were, but this is the feeling I got. I say we for as always I was accompanied by someone although I never know who! On the top of the eskers was a thin layer of grass which came a little ways down the sides. It was daylight and we walked up the gravel between the two eskers for a short distance, we stopped and ahead of us crouching behind a few large boulders were a Mother and child Sasquatch. How do I know this? Well it is quite obvious once you see them! I remember looking at them from a distance of about twenty feet; we just stood and looked at each other. After a few minutes the mother stood up, looked at us and smiled. I remember being enveloped in a warmth and serenity not felt before, this was emanating from the Sasquatch and made me feel very calm and relaxed. I remember smiling at them and waving. This was received with a warm and somehow knowing smile. I am sure they knew we were coming as I am told visits to Sasquatch are virtually unheard of as they are a very private and highly spiritual race.

As I looked at the two of them, basking in their spiritual light. I tried to get a good look at them, especially the mother. She was covered in a light red or maybe light shining ginger hair, similar to the colour of an Orangutan, but with a definite shine to it. The face was devoid of hair in a kind of circle about the face. The skin was a pale beige colour and she looked remarkably like a human except for a wider bridge on the nose. She did not look like an Orangutan but much, much more closer to a human with beautiful eyes, although I cannot remember what colour they were, they just sparkled. I remember how radiant and serene she looked in the face. I remember a glow about the body which you don't see in humans. This race which I am told is spiritually many levels higher than the human. I cannot forget the glow surrounding them, an aura of brightness so gentle on the eyes. I did not really look at the child much as I was so captivated by the beauty of the mother. She seemed to be one or two feet taller than me. It was hard to tell as they were behind the boulder hidden from the waist down.

It must have been only a few minutes before I got the impression we were about to leave. I waved and the mother waved back. I did not get any closer as I did not really need to. I smiled, said "thank you" and we left. The next thing I remember is waking up and going over in my mind what a special visit I had just been on. Will I ever see them again? I do not know, but I won't forget the spiritual serenity that came from them.

So - Sasquatch hunters - stop trying to hunt them! I do not understand why humans are so obsessed with hunting and killing beings of all types for sport, whether it be in the air, on the water or on land. There are not very many Sasquatch left on this world. Hundreds of years ago all natives around the world were taught to respect and live in harmony with the Sasquatch. So please make an effort to leave them alone in peace in their peaceful world! They are more spiritual than us humans will ever be!

O' Great Spirit

O' GREAT SPIRIT
Whose voice I hear in the wind, and whose breath gives life to all the world,
Hear me! I am small and weak, I need your strength and wisdom.
Let me walk in beauty, and make my eyes ever behold the red and purple sunset.
Make my hands respect the things you have made and my eyes sharp to hear your voice.
Make me wise so that I may understand the things you have taught my people.
Help me to remain calm and strong in the face of all that comes towards me.
Let me learn the lessons you have hidden in every leaf and rock.
Help me seek pure thoughts and act with the intention of helping others.
Help me find compassion without empathy over whelming me.
I seek strength, not to be greater than my brother, but to fight my greatest enemy - myself!
Make me always ready to come to you with clean hands and straight eyes.
So when life fades, as the fading sunset, my spirit may come to you without shame.

By Unknown Native American Chief and M.J. Shutt

Made in the USA
Columbia, SC
06 April 2018